MOTIVATOR

In Sync 3

Clare Maxwell

PEARSON
Longman

In Sync 3 Motivator

Authorized adaptation from the United Kingdom edition, entitled *Upbeat*, first edition, published by Pearson Education Limited publishing under its Longman imprint. Copyright © 2009.

American English adaptation, published by Pearson Education, Inc. Copyright © 2011.

Pearson Education, 10 Bank Street, White Plains, NY 10606, USA

Staff credits: The people who made up the *In Sync* team, representing editorial, production, design, and manufacturing, are Margaret Antonini, Danielle Belfiore, Iris Candelaria, Aerin Csigay, Dave Dickey, Ann France, Lisa Ghiozzi, Emily Lippincott, Leslie Patterson, Stella Reilly, Mary Rich, Barbara Sabella, Donna Schaffer, Julie Schmidt, Mairead Stack, Jennifer Stem, Katherine Sullivan, Jane Townsend, Paula Van Ells, Lauren Weidenman, and Adina Zoltan.

Text composition: TSI Graphics
Text font: Helvetica Neue 10/17

ISBN-13: 978-0-13-254807-6
ISBN-10: 0-13-254807-0

PEARSON LONGMAN ON THE **WEB**

Pearsonlongman.com offers online resources for teachers. Access our Companion Websites, our online catalog, and our local offices around the world.

Visit us at **pearsonlongman.com**.

Printed in the United States of America
1 2 3 4 5 6 7 8 9 10—V012—15 14 13 12 11

Photo credits: All original photography by TSI Graphics and Pearson Education Limited/Gareth Boden.
Cover: Shutterstock.com. Page 2 (1) Thinkstock Royalty-Free, (2) iStockphoto.com, (3) iStockphoto.com, (4) iStockphoto.com; 22 iStockphoto.com; 23 KPA/Zuma/Rex Features; 31 Giuliano Bevilacqua/Rex Features; 33 (top) AFP/Getty Images, (bottom) NBCUPHOTOBANK/Rex Features; 41 Thinkstock Royalty-Free; 50 (top) Andreas Pollok/Getty Images, (bottom) Leland Bobbe/Getty Images.

Illustration credits: Illustrations throughout by Advocate.
Artists: Martin Goneau, Anita Romeo, Susan Tait Porcaro.

Contents

1A What's your personality?

1 Unscramble the adjectives in the personality profiles.

ARIES: March 21–April 20

You are very [1] _sociable_ (BELCOSIA): you love parties! You have a lot of friends, because you are [2] _____ (FRYLINED) and [3] _____ (SAYE-GINGO). But on bad days, you are very [4] _____ (DAB-DEMERPET)!!

GEMINI: May 22–June 21

You are usually calm and [5] _____ (EXARELD). You have a lot of friends because you are very [6] _____ (ONGESEUR), and [7] _____ (VETSNISIE). But sometimes you can become [8] _____ (YOMOD).

VIRGO: August 22–September 23

You like studying, and you do well at school because you are very [9] _____ (LINTIGELTEN), but you are not very [10] _____ (FLES-TONFINCED).You don't often go out because you are quite [11] _____ (YHS).

SAGITTARIUS: November 23–December 22

You like adventure, but you want results now! You are very [12] _____ (TIMPANITE). And you usually make good decisions because you are quite a [13] _____ (BINELESS), but you are sometimes [14] _____ (SOBSY).

2 Look at the dates and match the zodiac signs and profiles to the people.

Sara: April 7
1 _____

Marcus: December 19
2 _____

Alex: June 3
3 _____

Dave: September 20
4 _____

3 Write the name of Sara's ideal friend. Give reasons for your answer.

Sara's ideal friend is _____ because _____.

1B Where are you?

1 Read the instant messages between Emilio and Alicia. Complete the sentences with the words in the box.

Alicia ⬚◻✕

Conversation Options Send To

| 👤 **Alicia** ✕ | 👤 **Moviefone** ✕ |

👤 **Alicia**

(04:25:46 PM) **alicia:** Hey, Emilio! Where are you today?
(04:25:48 PM) **emilio:** I'm in Denver!
(04:25:53 PM) **alicia:** (1) _____'s Denver?
(04:25:57 PM) **emilio:** It's in Colorado—in the mountains.
(04:26:03 PM) **alicia:** So …(2) _____'s it like there?
(04:26:07 PM) **emilio:** Amazing! There's so much to do here!
(04:26:09 PM) **alicia:** (3) _____ are you coming home?
(04:26:13 PM) **emilio:** (4) _____ wants to know?
(04:26:15 PM) **alicia:** Me, stupid!
(04:26:19 PM) **emilio:** (5) _____?
(04:26:22 PM) **alicia:** Because I miss you!!

A Font | 🖌 Reset font | 😊 Insert

| what | when | where | who | why |

2 Alicia and Emilio start chatting at 4:25 and 46 seconds. How long do they talk?

_____ seconds

1c What's my job?

1 Look at the picture clues and complete the crossword puzzle.

Across

Down

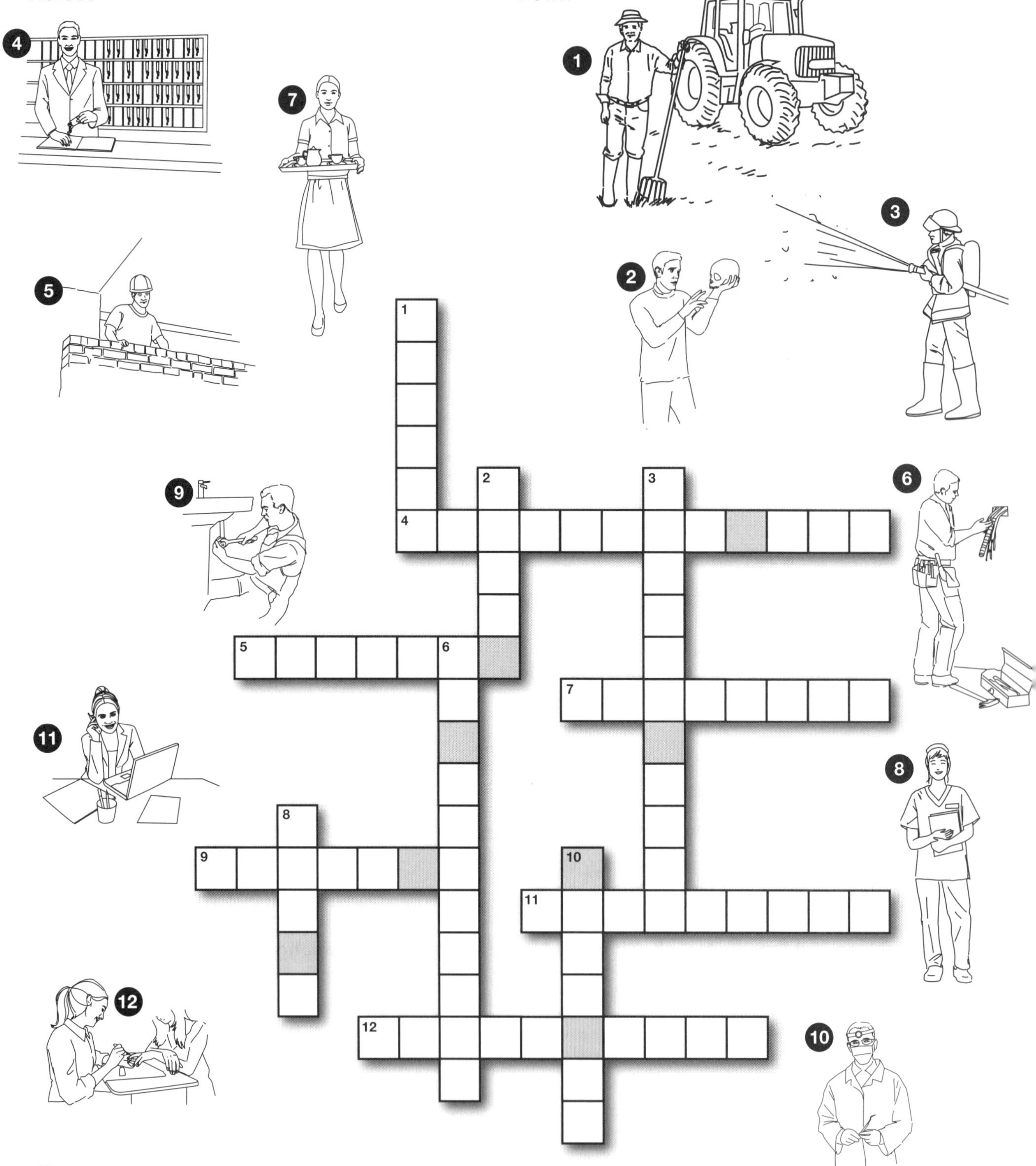

2 Write the letters from the highlighted squares in the boxes.
Then unscramble the letters to find the hidden job.

An evening at the movies

1 Write the appropriate question word(s) for each question. Then write questions a–h in the correct speech bubbles.

Who	What
Where	~~What time~~
Why	What type
How long	How much

a) *What time* does the movie start?

b) _____ does it cost?

c) _____ 's in it?

d) _____ are you going, Matt?

e) _____ of movie is it?

f) _____ is it?

g) _____ movie is playing?

h) _____ don't you come?

1

1 _____

To the movies, Sam.

2

2 _____

The new James Bond movie.

3

3 _____

It's an adventure movie.

4

4 _____

Daniel Craig.

5

5 *What time does the movie start?*

At seven thirty.

6

6 _____

About two hours.

7

7 _____

I think tickets are about $8.

8

8 _____

I'd love to, but . . .

2 Invent Sam's reply to Matt's question in picture 8. _____

1 Inspector Ryan is investigating a murder at Hogbury Hall. Read the police officer's notes and complete the witness statements with the correct form of the verbs.

Police Officer Plod

When I arrived at 7:45 P.M., the victim was on the floor in the kitchen, near the back door. There was a knife near the man's body, but there wasn't any blood.

Doctor Paul

I ¹*was walking* (walk) to the dining room when I ²_____ (see) Susie Blue. She was running up the stairs. She ³_____ (have) an unusual blue bottle in her hand. It was about 7:25 P.M.

Alice Ackerley

At 7:30, Mrs. Mop ⁴_____ (make) dinner, and I ⁵_____ (clean) the candlesticks in the dining room when I ⁶_____ (hear) a scream. I immediately ⁷_____ (run) to the kitchen. Mrs. Mop ⁸_____ (stand) near the door, looking at a body. It was the master of the house!

Dirty Den

At around 7 P.M. I was with Mr. Rogers in the garage. He ⁹_____ (clean) his gun, and I ¹⁰_____ (look for) a bottle of rat poison, but I didn't find it. At about 7:20 P.M. Mr. Rogers ¹¹_____ (leave) the garage to go for dinner.

Susie Blue

I ¹²_____ (wash) my hair in the bathroom upstairs when I ¹³_____ (hear) the police car outside, so I ¹⁴_____ (go) downstairs. While I ¹⁵_____ (run) downstairs I ¹⁶_____ (notice) Doctor Paul in the hall, near the entrance to the kitchen.

Possible method

| gun | knife | poison | candlestick |

2 One of the witnesses is lying and is the murderer. Read the statements again and answer the questions.

1 Who is the victim? _____

2 Who is the murderer? _____

3 What did the murderer use to commit the murder? _____

2A Battle of the bands

1 Circle the odd word in each group of words.

1 podcast   webcast   (band)   concert
2 gig   MP3 player   CD player   recorder
3 techno   soul   radio   folk
4 playlist   reggae   hip-hop   country
5 download   piano   trumpet   drums

6 flute   saxophone   cello   clarinet
7 violin   guitar   trumpet   cello
8 musician   instrument   performer   producer
9 trumpet   drums   clarinet   saxophone
10 acoustic   piano   bass   lead

2 Write the odd words from Exercise 1 in the box. Then use the words to complete the interview below.

> band,

I: Today on *Music Box* we are interviewing a local musician, Mark Janes. Hi, Mark. So, tell us about your musical activities.

M: Well, I'm in a ¹*band* called *XYZ* with some of my friends. I'm the keyboard player because I can also play the ² _____, which is a very similar ³_____.

I: And where do you practice?

M: Well, Jake plays the ⁴_____. We usually practice in his dad's garage so we don't disturb the neighbors!

I: Do you perform in public?

M: We're going to play our first ⁵_____ on Saturday. We're going to be in the *Battle of the Bands* competition.

I: That will give you good publicity.

M: Yes. The competition is going to be live on the ⁶_____, and I hope there'll be a podcast so I can ⁷_____ it from the Internet.

I: Does your family share your passion for music?

M: Oh, yes. My sister Susie plays the ⁸_____ in a local jazz band. My younger brother is into classical music. He plays the ⁹_____ in the school orchestra.

I: And what kind of music do you like?

M: All sorts. I like rock, pop, hip-hop, and techno. When I'm not playing music, I'm listening to it on my MP3 player. I've created over 50 different ¹⁰_____s.

I: Wow! So, what are your plans for the future?

M: That's easy. I'm going to be a professional musician!

What are you doing on Saturday?

Student A

Look at the poster and your calendar. Find out Student B's plans for the weekend, and find a time to go to the movies together. Write the time into your calendar.

A: Would you like to go to see *The Deep* on Friday evening?

B: I'm afraid I can't. I'm . . .

A: OK, what are you doing on . . . ?

THE ODEON

The Deep

Friday and Saturday
at
2:30 and 4:45

Special viewing!

Sunday at 11:00 A.M.

Friday 27th
Basketball tournament
2-4 P.M.

Saturday 28th
Jake's birthday!!
11 A.M.: quad-biking with Jake
12:30: birthday pizza for Jake

Sunday 29th

3 P.M.: visit Grandad in hospital

✂ -

Student B

Look at the poster and your calendar. Find out Student A's plans for the weekend and find a time to go bowling together. Write the time into your calendar.

B: Would you like to go bowling on Friday afternoon?

A: I'm afraid I can't. I'm . . .

B: OK, what are you doing on . . . ?

Westlane Bowling Alley

Bowling Tournaments
Fridays, Saturdays, and Sundays
2 P.M. – 5 P.M.

All are welcome!
Call us to book a one-hour game

Friday 27th
2:00 P.M.: pizza with Dave

Saturday 28th
11 A.M.: meet Jo in town to buy present for Sal

9 P.M.: Sal's 18th birthday party

Sunday 29th

4 P.M.: coffee in town with Steve

2C Movie reviews

1 Read the movie reviews and complete the words.

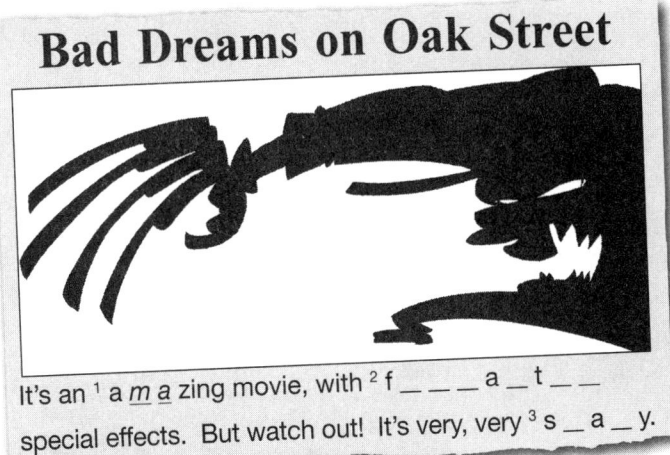

Bad Dreams on Oak Street

It's an [1] a _m a_ zing movie, with [2] f _ _ _ a _ t _ _ special effects. But watch out! It's very, very [3] s _ a _ y.

When Larry Met Allie

Aaah! It's a movie that warms your heart. It's funny and [10] s _ _ at the same time. Unfortunately there are some [11] d _ l _ moments, but it has a beautiful, happy ending.

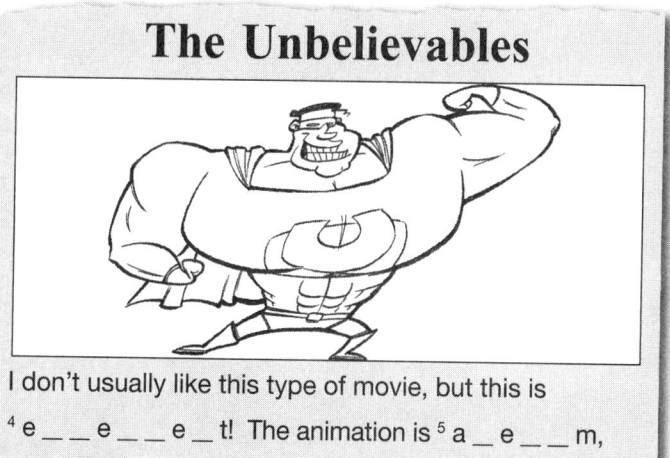

The Unbelievables

I don't usually like this type of movie, but this is [4] e _ _ _ e _ _ e _ t! The animation is [5] a _ e _ _ m, and the story is very [6] _ mu _ _ _ _ g.

Low Morning

This movie is the worst. The story is [7] c _ nf _ _ _ n _ : it's difficult to understand what's happening, and the actors are [8] t _ rr _ _ _ l _. It's the usual, [9] b _ _ i _ g story of cowboys and Indians.

2 Unscramble the actors' names to find the movie categories. Then say which actors star in which movies.

1 Nat Coro   _cartoon: The Unbelievables_

2 Ern West   _____

3 R.H. Roor   _____

4 Tom Carin Medcoy _____

Choose the correct answer. Check your answers and write your score.

1 Which famous singer has not starred in a Hollywood movie?
   a) Madonna   **b)** Robbie Williams   **c)** Eminem

2 Which of these actors is the shortest?
   a) Tom Cruise   **b)** Danny DeVito   **c)** Arnold Schwarzenegger

3 Which of these actresses is the tallest?
   a) Julia Roberts   **b)** Cameron Diaz   **c)** Nicole Kidman

4 Which of these movies is not from a book?
   a) *The Lord of the Rings*   **b)** *Pirates of the Caribbean*   **c)** *Bridget Jones' Diary*

5 Which of these actors has won the most Oscars?
   a) Orlando Bloom   **b)** Leonardo DiCaprio   **c)** Robert De Niro

6 Which country produces the most movies every year?
   a) the U.S.   **b)** India   **c)** China

7 Which of these actors is the oldest?
   a) Joey King   **b)** Kristen Stewart   **c)** Daniel Radcliffe

8 Which of these movies was the most expensive to make?
   a) *Titanic*   **b)** *Avatar*   **c)** *Spiderman 3*

My score: _____

7–8	Wow! You're a movie expert!
5–6	You know a lot about movies.
2–4	You're not very interested in movies.
0–1	You're a very, very serious person!

1 Marcia is a very busy woman. Look at her calendar and complete her responses in the speech bubbles.

1 Would you like to go to the movies on Monday afternoon?

I'm sorry, I can't. I'm ¹ *meeting my agent* on Monday.

2 Do you want to go to a play on Tuesday evening?

I'd like to, but ² _____ on Tuesday.

3 Do you want to have lunch with me on Wednesday?

That would be great, but ³ _____ on Wednesday.

4 Would you like to go bowling on Thursday evening?

I'm sorry, but ⁴ _____ on Thursday.

Mon	3 P.M.: Meet my agent
Tues	Go to Gwyneth's party
Wed	12:30 P.M.: Play tennis
Thur	Have dinner with the Beckhams
Fri	FREE!

2 Look at the final picture and complete the man's response.

5 What about Friday? Would you like to take me out on Friday?

I ⁵ _____, but _____ on Friday!

3A Cleaning up!

1 Sam has invited some friends for dinner this evening, but his apartment is a mess! Look at the pictures of his apartment at 11 A.M. and 5 P.M. and find the differences.

Use the "To Do" list to describe the differences. Use the present perfect and *yet / already,* if appropriate.

To do

Do the laundry	Feed the cat
Clean the stove	Make the bed
Vacuum	Empty the trash
Do the ironing	Wash the dishes

A 11 A.M.

B 5 P.M.

1 *Sam hasn't done the laundry yet.*   *He's done the laundry.*

2 _____.   _____.

3 _____.   _____.

4 _____.   _____.

5 _____.   _____.

6 _____.   _____.

7 _____.   _____.

2 It's 5 P.M. What hasn't he done yet? _____

Yes! magazine

1 Read the article and fill in the blanks with the correct form of the verbs from the box.

have arguments	ask somebody out	~~get divorced~~	break up	make up
meet	be married	get married	be engaged to	get engaged

>>>BREAKING NEWS – BREAKING NEWS – BREAKING NEWS <<<

Hollywood's favorite couple, Liam Henshall and Allie Carney, [1] *have gotten divorced*! The Liam–Allie relationship has become one of the most famous in Hollywood. They [2] _____ in public many times since their wedding two years ago, and they [3] _____ four times. Up to now, they always [4] _____ afterward, but not this time.

The couple [5] _____ for the first time three years ago on the set of the movie *True Love*. Liam liked Allie immediately and he [6] _____ on the first day of filming. It was a dream romance, but it shocked Hollywood because at that time, Liam [7] _____ to actress Mia Rooney and Allie [8] _____ movie producer Ray Bradberg. Bradberg canceled the wedding, and Rooney and Liam got divorced.

Liam and Allie [9] _____ after a month, exchanging rings that cost over $200,000, and a year later they [10] _____. But things soon changed, as work and personal differences caused problems between the couple. Now it seems the dream is over.

2 Write the answers to the questions. Use the highlighted letters to discover the mystery word.

1 What was the title of Liam and Allie's first movie together? ☐ _ _ _   _ _ _ _
2 Where do Liam and Allie work? ☐ _ _ _ _ _ _ _ _
3 What was Mia Rooney's relationship to Liam? _ ☐ _ _
4 What was Ray Bradberg's job? _ ☐ _ ☐ _ _ _

3 Complete the instruction with the mystery word.

Circle every _____ word.

wedding	make	year	wife	on	married	London	date	couples	to
well	every	engaged	woman	sixty	give	ring	thousand	Hollywood	
actor	get	husband	argue	Vegas	cake	never	Las	divorce	is	in

4 Reorder the circled words to discover the mystery fact!

_____ _____ _____ _____

_____ _____ _____

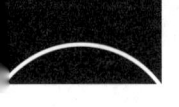

3c Happy families

1 Read the clues below and complete the family tree.

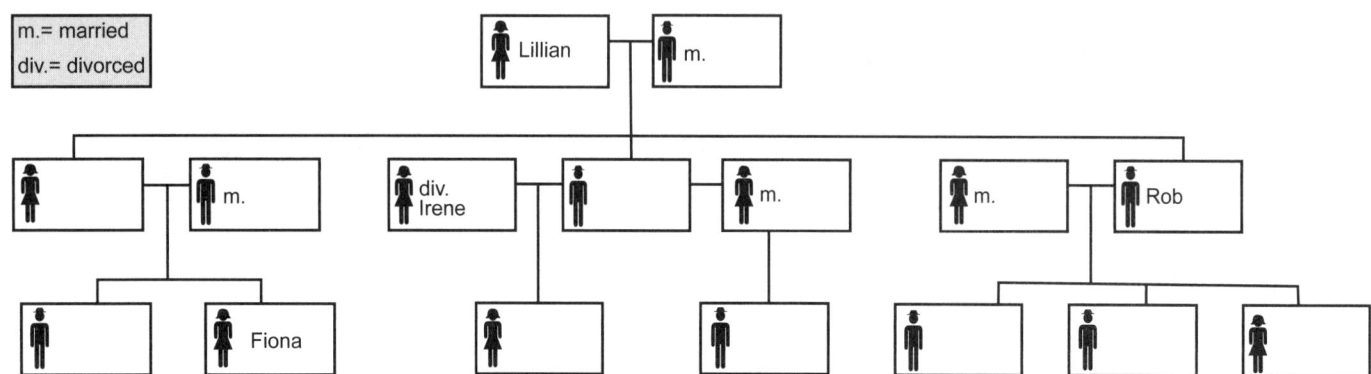

1. John has three children and seven grandchildren.
2. Jeremy is Rob's brother.
3. Sally has one son and no daughters.
4. Sally and Jean are John and Lillian's daughters-in-law.
5. Jessica is Nick's step-sister.
6. Julia and Peter are married.
7. Jessica is Rob's niece.
8. Debbie has four cousins and two brothers. One of her brothers is named Dave.
9. Neil has one brother. He is Fiona's cousin.
10. Steve is Jeremy's nephew.

2 Read the e-mail. Who is it from?

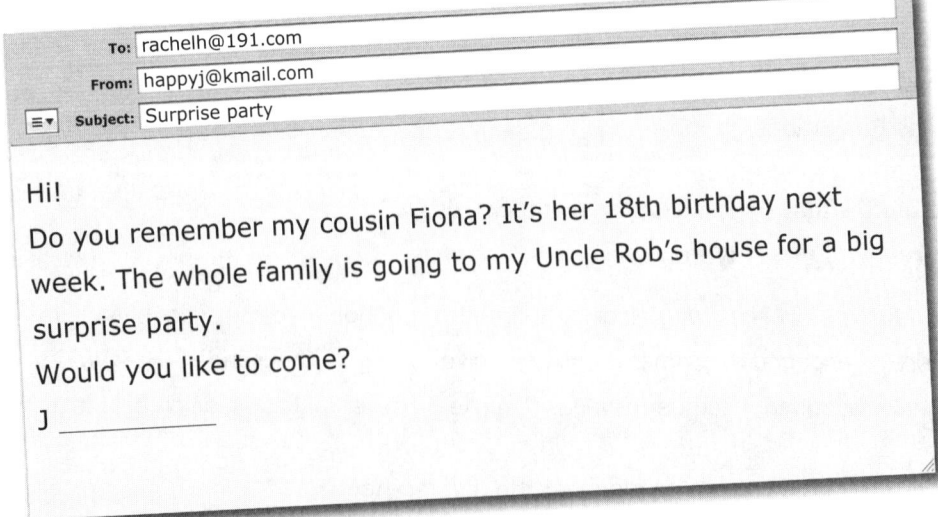

To: rachelh@191.com
From: happyj@kmail.com
Subject: Surprise party

Hi!
Do you remember my cousin Fiona? It's her 18th birthday next week. The whole family is going to my Uncle Rob's house for a big surprise party.
Would you like to come?
J _____

What's the matter?

The last lines of the conversations have been mixed up. Complete the conversations with the correct form of the verbs, then match the last lines to the correct conversations.

1

A: You look miserable. What's the matter?

B: I've just [1] *gotten* (get) my test results.

 I've [2] _____ (fail) them all.

A: Oh dear. Well, why don't you take them again?

B: He [3] _____ (be) with my girlfriend! ☐

2

A: You look upset. What's the matter?

B: I've just [4] _____ (see) my best friend.

A: Oh! So, what's the problem?

B: I've already [5] _____ (look) there. It's disappeared! ☐

3

A: You look worried. What's the matter?

B: I've [6] _____ (lose) my digital camera. My parents [7] _____ (give) it to me for my birthday last year.

A: I see. Well, why don't you look for it in your bedroom?

B: I've already [8] _____ (take) them five times! ☐

Clauses crossword puzzle

Across

5 The object that you use to open a locked door.
6 A place where you can buy food.
7 A red light means _____ .
9 A thing that you wear on your foot.
11 A person who works in a hospital.
12 When people are angry and shout, they have an _____ .

Down

1 Something that you eat between meals when you are hungry.
2 The relative who is married to your sister.
3 The meal that you eat in the morning.
4 The part of your body where you wear a hat.
5 The place where you usually cook a meal.
8 Schoolwork that you do at home.
10 The ceremony that people have when they get married.

4A   A busy day

1 You stopped at many places today. Look at the pictures and write the places you went to.

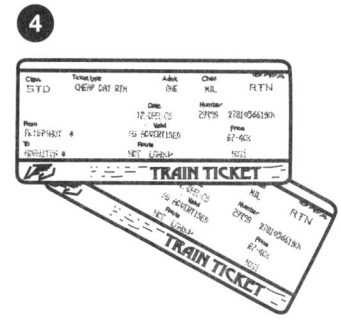   

1 __ __ [2] __ __ __ __ __ __

2 __ __ __ [8] __ __ __ __ __

3 __ [6] __ __ [9] __ __ __ __ __

4 __ __ __ __ __ __ [5] __ __ __ __ __

5 [4] __ __ __ [7] __ __ __ __ __

6 [1] __ __ __

7 __ __ __ __ __ [3] __

2 Write the highlighted letters in the correct square below. (Use the numbers in the boxes to help you.) Where did you forget to go? Complete the sentence.

I forgot to go to the _____ to [1] [2] [3] [4] [5] [6] [7 m] [8] [9] .

4B Your perfect room!

1 You have to buy some furniture for your new attic bedroom. You need a wardrobe or stand-alone closet, a desk, and a chair. Look at the room plan and draw the items you choose on the plan.

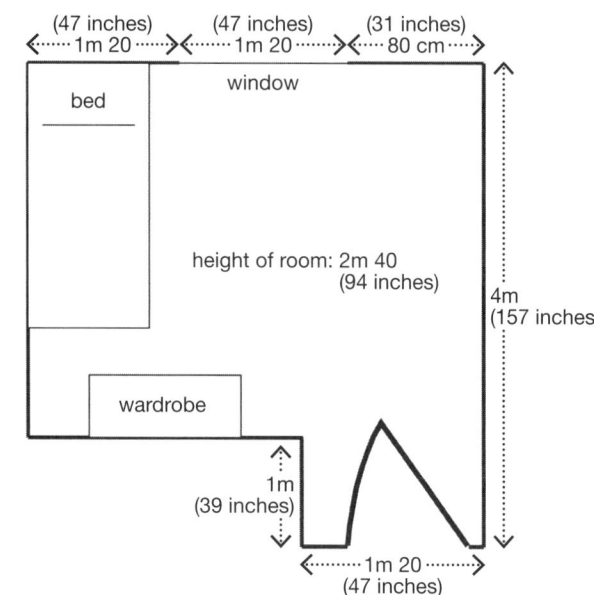

Wardrobes (Stand-alone closets)

1 Easyfix

2 Flatpack

3 Chesterton

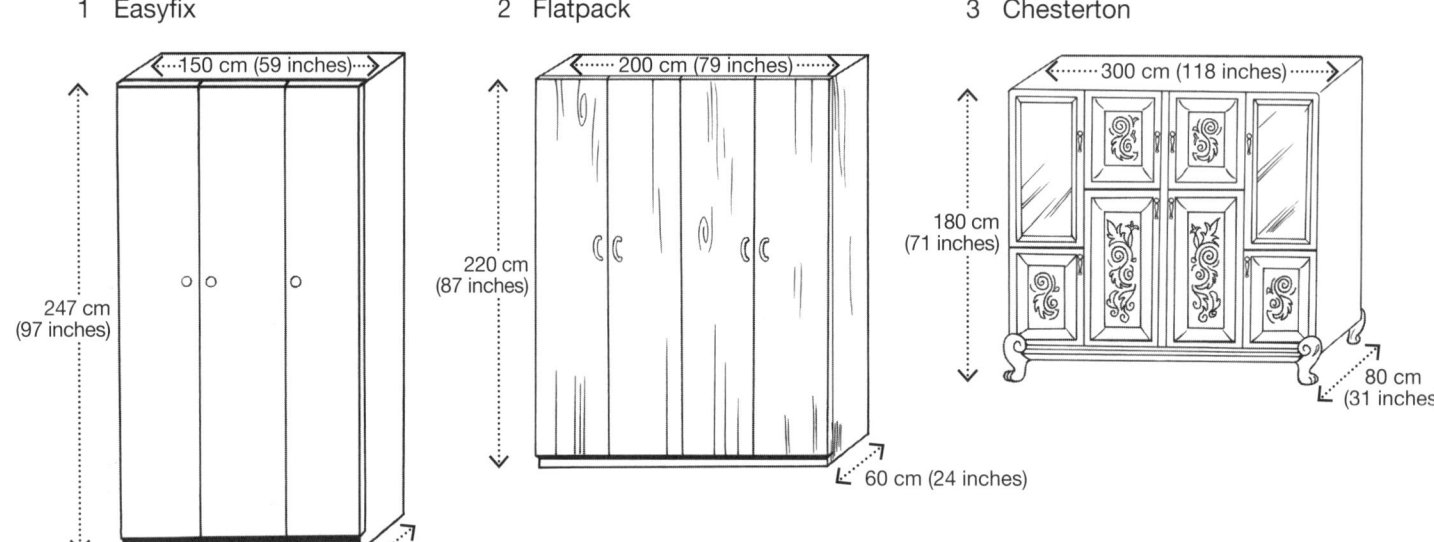

Desks and chairs

1 Easydesk

2 Antique

3 Spacemaster

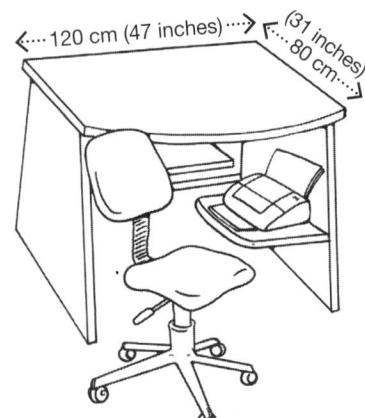

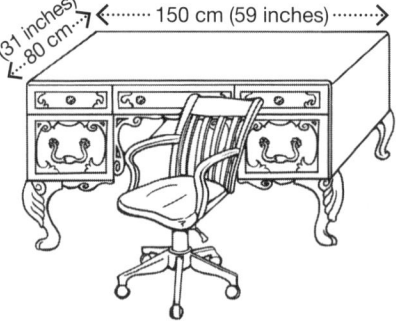

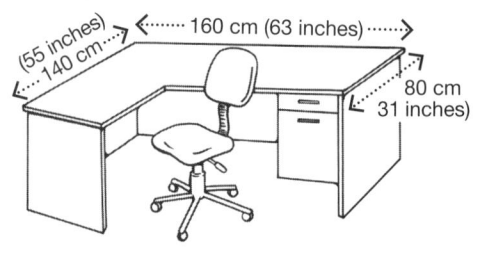

2 Tell the class which furniture you are going to buy and explain your choices.

We're going to buy . . .

We're not going to buy . . . because it's too . . .

The waiting room

Read the story and complete the sentences in the speech bubbles using *too much/too many* or *not enough*.

1
. . . because I can't sleep at night. There ¹*'s too much noise* (noise).

2
I agree. And there ² _____ (pollution). That's why I'm here.

3
Forty minutes on the bus! There ³ _____ (traffic) in this town.

4
He's right you know. There ⁴ _____ (people), that's the problem.

5
That's right. And those young people with their fast cars! They've got ⁵ _____ (money) in my opinion.

6
And there ⁶ _____ (not respect). I remember years ago . . .

7
Excuse me, is there a problem?

Yes. My music ⁷ _____ (not loud)!

Can you tell me how to get to . . . ?

Student A

1 You are at the train station. Look at your To Do list. Identify where you need to go and write the places on the list.

2 Ask Student B for directions to each place. Start from the train station each time.

A: Can you tell me how to get to . . . ?
B: Yes, go left out of the train station parking lot, turn left on . . .

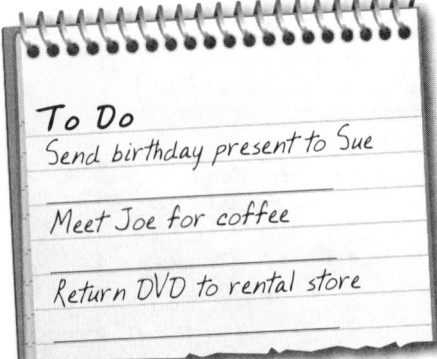

To Do
Send birthday present to Sue

Meet Joe for coffee

Return DVD to rental store

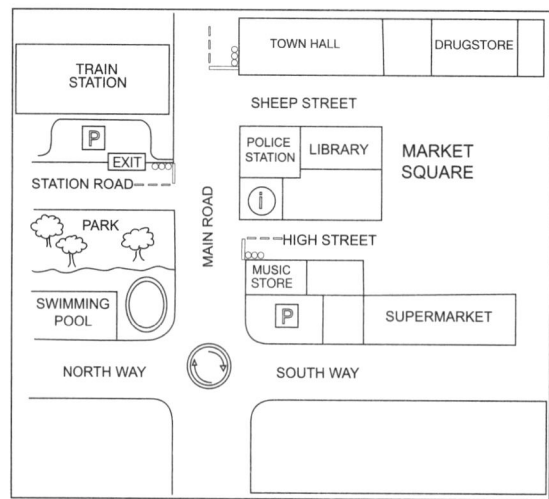

3 Give Student B directions to the places he/she asks for, starting from the train station.

✂ -

Student B

1 You are at the train station. Look at your To Do list. Identify where you need to go and write the places on the list.

2 Give Student A directions to the places he/she asks for, starting from the train station.

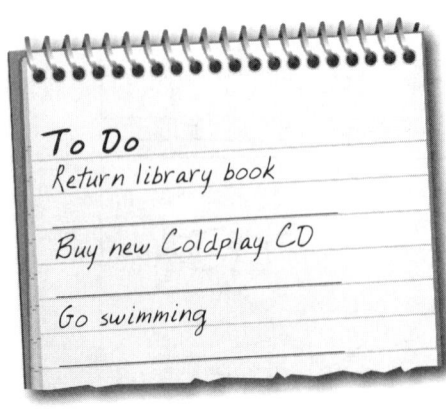

To Do
Return library book

Buy new Coldplay CD

Go swimming

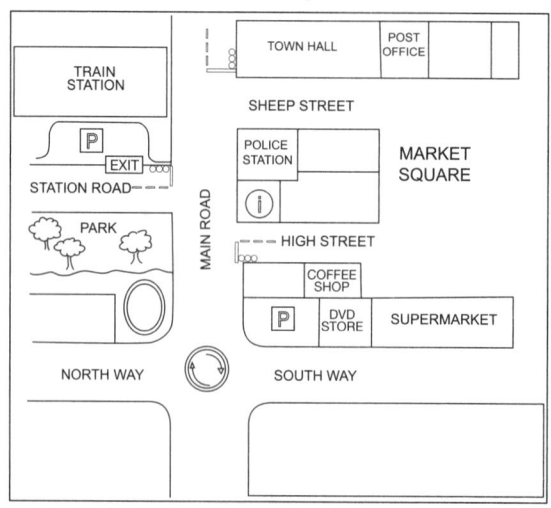

3 Then ask Student A for directions to each place. Start from the train station each time.

A: Can you tell me how to get to . . . ?
B: Yes, go left out of the train station parking lot, turn left on . . .

Look at Jo's tickets and receipts from her recent trip from England to New York.
Complete the details of her trip below and number them in the correct order.

Buses from Headington to Oxford train station

9:00   11:00   ~~1:00~~   3:00   5:00

296573
Liberty Ferry
June 28
1 round trip to Statue of Liberty
296573

CENTRAL PARK BIKE RENTAL
Friday June 29
$20

Big Smile Taxis
JFK to Chelsea Hotel, Manhattan
$45

C U at Hthrw Sun PM! I'll have new car! Dave x

FROM LONDON HEATHROW
TO JFK NEW YORK

FLIGHT 630

DEPART WEDNESDAY 06 27
4:45

FROM JFK NEW YORK
TO LONDON HEATHROW

FLIGHT 325

DEPART SUNDAY 07 01
10:15

ROYAL RAILROAD
From
OXFORD
To
LONDON PADDINGTON
SINGLE

ADMIT ONE | I could have **danced all night**
Evening performance
9 P.M., June 30

☐	JFK Airport to Manhattan by _____	1	Headington to the train station by ___bus___
☐	London to New York by _____	☐	Paddington station to Heathrow by _____
☐	Oxford to London by _____	☐	Return home from airport by _____
☐	Saturday evening show at _____		with _____
☐	See Central Park by _____	☐	Visit Statue of Liberty by _____

5A Organized chaos

1 Read about Susanna's day yesterday and fill in the blanks with the correct form of *make* or *do*.

SUSIE'S BLOG Today I'm feeling ☹

Phew! What an awful day today! I woke up with a toothache, so Mom [1] *made* an appointment with the dentist for this afternoon. I never have time for breakfast so I [2]_____ a quick cup of coffee—and then went to school. But I forgot my homework! I always [3]_____ my homework in the afternoon (so I can watch TV in the evening), but I forgot to put it in my bag. Before lunch we had a math test. It was really hard. I [4]_____ my best, but I know I [5]_____ lots of mistakes. I studied all last week for that test, but it [6]_____ no difference. In the evening I tried to [7]_____ a cake for my friend's birthday, but I [8]_____ a terrible mess of the kitchen. Now I'm really tired!

Tomorrow is a holiday: HOORAY! I'm going to sleep late and have a really lazy day.

2 Imagine you are Susanna. Complete the quiz for her.

HOW ORGANIZED ARE YOU?

1 When do you do your homework?
   a) immediately after school
   b) in the evening, after dinner
   c) on the bus in the morning

2 What is the first thing you do in the morning?
   a) exercise
   b) make breakfast and eat it quickly
   c) grab coffee, and run to school, late again!

3 You have a day off. What do you do?
   a) I get up early and do some yoga.
   b) I get up late then go out with friends.
   c) I get up late and do nothing all day.

4 Your mom has asked you to make a cake for your sister's birthday. What do you do?
   a) I make a beautiful cake and clean up.
   b) I buy a cake from the supermarket: it's the thought that counts.
   c) I do my best, but I make a mess!

Key

Mostly a): You are very well organized. You like to have your life under control.

Mostly b): You are somewhat organized, particularly about important things, but sometimes you make mistakes.

Mostly c): Your life is chaos! Can you remember your name?

3 Complete the quiz for yourself. Then compare your results with another student.

The world's most famous spy!

Student A

1 Use the cues to ask Student B questions to complete the article. Answer Student B's questions.

James Bond is the most famous spy in the world. Ian Fleming wrote the first Bond book in ¹ _____ (*when?*). Since then, the books have sold more than 100 million copies. People have been watching Bond movies for more than 40 years. ⁴ _____ (*how many?*) different actors have played James Bond since the movies began in 1962.

Daniel Craig is ⁶ _____ (*what/doing?*) at the moment. He has been in Italy f(o)r a mo(n)th. Daniel and the film crew have been traveling around Italy ⁸ _____ (*how long?*). They've already filmed scenes in Sie(n)a and (R)ome. Now they're at Lake Garda. They've been ¹⁰ _____ (*what/do?*) around the lake, including a ¹¹ _____ (*what?*)! Daniel Craig has been acting in movies for nearly 20 (y)ears. He's been playing James Bond ¹⁴ _____ (*how long?*).

2 Look at the circled letters in the article. Write them below. Ask Student B for his/her circled letters and add them in.

☐ ☐ ☐ ☐ ☐ ☐ ☐ ☐ ☐ ☐ ☐

Unscramble the letters to answer this question: Who was the first James Bond actor? _____

✂ -

Student B

1 Answer Student A's questions. Use the cues to ask Student A questions to complete the article.

James Bond is the most famous spy in the world. Ian Fleming wrote the first Bond book in 1952. Since then, the books have sold ² _____ (*how many?*) copies. People have been watching Bond movies for ³ _____ (*how long?*). (S)ix different actors have played James Bond since the movies began ⁵ _____ (*when?*). Daniel Craig is filming the l(a)test James Bond movie at the moment. He has been in Italy ⁷ _____ (*how long?*). Daniel and the movie crew have been traveling around Italy si(n)ce February. They've already filmed scenes in ⁹ _____ (*where?*). Now they're at Lake Garda. They've been driving v(e)ry fast (c)ars around the lake, including a very (e)xpensive Aston Martin car! Daniel Craig has been acting in movies for ¹² _____ (*how long?*). He's been playing James Bond since 2006.

2 Look at the circled letters in the article. Write them below. Ask Student A for his/her circled letters and add them in.

☐ ☐ ☐ ☐ ☐ ☐ ☐ ☐ ☐ ☐ ☐

Unscramble the letters to answer this question: Who was the first actor to play James Bond in the movies? _____

5c Eating out

1 Unscramble the letters to complete the menus.

MENU 1

Starters
Stufled [1] *mushrooms* (ROSHOMUMS)

[2] _____ (PRIMSH) cocktail

Main Courses, *served with*
[3] _____ (DEAKB) or [4] _____ (SHAMED)

potatoes and a selection of fresh [5] _____

(BLEVATEGES)

[6] _____ (ATORS) lamb with mint sauce

[7]Grilled _____ (HINCECK)

Dessert
[8] _____ (WRESTRABRY) cheesecake

A choice of ice cream

MENU 2

[9] _____ **(WASHENDSIC)**

¾ lb. [10] _____ (GRUBER)

[11] _____ (LIRGELD) cheese

[12] _____ (AUNT) melt

Sides
[13]Small _____ (IFESR)

[14] _____ (RALCIG) bread

[15]mixed _____ (DALSA)

Dessert
[16] _____ (HOTCOLACE) cake

[17] _____ (PELPA) pie

MENU 3

Traditional dishes from the heart of the Mediterranean

[18] _____ (THASPIGEIT) bolognese

Vegetable [19] _____ (ASALGAN)

[20] _____ (TAME) ravioli in tomato sauce

Three–[21] _____ (HESECE) _____

[22](ZAPIZ)

2 Match the menus to the restaurants.

 **A** MENU ____

 **B** MENU ____

C MENU ____

1 Jessie, Ellie, Ray, and Andy went out for dinner last night.
Read the clues and look at the bill, and write what each person ate.

The Angel Inn
Restaurant

Starters

1	Shrimp cocktail	$5.95
1	Onion soup	$4.80
1	Stuffed mushrooms	$5.50

Main Courses

1	Salmon with roasted potatoes	$10.95
1	Steak and mashed potatoes	$9.90
1	Roast beef	$12.50
1	Vegetable pasta	$10.95

Side orders

2	Green salads @ $3.50	$7.00
1	Mixed salad	$4.50
1	Roasted vegetables	$4.50

Desserts

1	Chocolate cheesecake	$4.80
1	Fruit salad	$4.50
2	Apple pies @ $4.30	$8.60

TOTAL

$94.45

Ellie

Vegetable pasta

Jessie

Ray

Andy

- Jessie hates fish and seafood.
- Ellie doesn't eat fish or meat.
- Ray doesn't like potatoes.
- Andy only had two courses and a side order.
- Ray didn't have a mixed salad.
- Jessie likes chocolate.
- The men didn't order roasted vegetables.
- The pasta was delicious with a green salad.
- Ellie and Ray had the same dessert.
- The soup was perfect before the steak and mashed potatoes!

2 How much did each person spend?

Jessie $_____   Ray $_____   Ellie $_____   Andy $_____

Match the conversations to the pictures. Then fill in the blanks with the phrasal verbs in the box.

| look at | looking after | looking for | looking forward to | ~~looking up~~ |

a Ben: What are you doing, Grandma?
Grandma: I'm ¹ *looking up* the times of the cartoons on TV, Ben.

b Friend: What are you doing today?
Grandma: I'm ² _____ my grandson.

c Ben: Grandma! Grandma! ³ _____ me! I'm a superhero!!
Grandma: Yes, Ben . . . I see.

d Ben: What are you doing, Grandma?
Grandma: I'm ⁴ _____ your teddy bear, Ben.

e Friend: Do you want to go to the movies tonight?
Grandma: No thanks. Sorry, but I'm ⁵ _____ a quiet evening at home.

6A Rags to riches

1 Look at the pictures and complete the sentences, using *used to/didn't use to* and an appropriate verb from the list.

~~be~~   eat   have (x2)   meet   talk   wear

Jack Trotter's my name; pleased to meet you. I'm a millionaire! But I [1] *used to be* very poor a few years ago. A lottery ticket changed my life forever. See this car? I [2] _____ a car like this—my last car was an old truck.

Oh yes, my life was so different. I [3] _____ old clothes, but now I have designer clothes. I [4] _____ any money. Now I can buy what I want. I go to a different restaurant every night. Before, I [5] _____ on a bench in the park. The best thing was that every afternoon I [6] _____ my friends on the street corner. We [7] _____ and laugh and tell stories. I miss that!

2 Write the word that comes *before* each given word in the text. Then fill in the blanks with the words to complete a summary of Jack's story.

1 *lottery* ticket   2 _____ restaurant   3 _____ forever   4 _____ a few

Lottery winner Trotter used to be _____. His _____ is very _____ now.

27

6B Modern-day hero

1 **Use the simple past form of the verbs in the box to complete the sentences.**

| carry | climb | fall | ~~jump~~ | push | swim | trip |

a) A woman _____ open the window. He _____ off the ladder.

b) The street was dark. He ran and _____ over a cat.

c) Donald was excited. He ran out of the house and *jumped* over the garden wall.

d) He _____ the flowers in his mouth and _____ across the river.

e) He ran to her house and found a ladder. He _____ up the ladder.

2 **Now match the sentences to the pictures to make the story.**

Picture	Sentence
1	c
2	
3	

Picture	Sentence
4	
5	

6c Mixed-up stories

The *Daily Press* recently interviewed two people, but their stories are mixed up.
Read the sentences and write the stories under the correct headlines below.
There are five sentences in each story.

Suddenly there was a loud CRASH outside. ☐

The woman was laughing and crying at the same time. ☐

A bus had crashed into the side of our house. ☐

Last month, my brother was at the mall. A1

I ran outside into the street. ☐

Last Thursday night I was in my room. ☐

She had won $10,000,000 in the lottery! ☐

He turned and saw a woman holding a piece of paper. ☐

Suddenly he heard a loud SCREAM. ☐

Fortunately nobody was hurt. ☐

A

$10 million winner!

Last month, my brother was at . . .

B

BUS HITS HOUSE

Complete the crossword puzzle with the missing words from the sentences.

Across

3 We had to stop and ask someone for directions because we'd lost our _____.

5 I'm losing _____ in my job. I'd like to try something new.

6 They were tired, so they _____ their bikes up the hill.

7 He couldn't tell the police anything about the accident because he'd lost his _____.

10 Edmund Hillary was the first man to _____ to the top of Mount Everest.

11 "My dad went to school with Robbie Williams!" "Wow! That's so _____!"

Down

1 I lost _____ of the people at the party, there were so many!

2 I _____ my cell phone on the floor and it broke.

3 "Would you like some cake?" "No thanks, I'm trying to lose _____."

4 My teacher really lost her _____ when I didn't turn in my homework.

8 The team played very well, but unfortunately lost the _____.

9 This is box is very heavy, I can't _____ it.

10 "Where's Sam?" "I haven't got a _____."

Student A

Use the cues to ask Student B questions to complete the article.

This week's Star Focus is on Rafael Nadal, the Spanish tennis champion.

Rafael Nadal was born on [1] *June 3, 1986* (*when?*) in Mallorca, Spain. Rafael ("Rafa") started playing tennis when he was [3] _____ (*how old?*). As a child he used to play tennis twice a week at his local club.

Rafa's manager, [5] _____ (*who?*), knew that Rafa had great talent. He was able to play with his left and his right hand, and he could run very fast. He became European Champion [7] _____ (*when?*), and when he was 14, he beat past champion Pat Cash.

Rafa has won nine Grand Slam titles and has won over [10] _____ (*how many?*) titles in all, including an Olympic Gold Medal.

✂ -

Student B

Use the cues to ask Student A questions to complete the article.

This week's Star Focus is on Rafael Nadal, the Spanish tennis champion.

Rafael Nadal was born on June 3, 1986 in [2] *Mallorca, Spain* (*where?*). Rafael ("Rafa") started playing tennis when he was three years old. As a child he used to play tennis [4] _____ (*how often?*) at his local club.

Rafa's manager, his uncle Toni, knew that Rafa had great talent. He was able to play [6] _____ (*how?*), and he could run very fast. He became European Champion when he was 12 years old; and when he was 14, he beat [8] _____ (*who?*).

Rafa has won [9] _____ (*how many?*) Grand Slam titles and has won over 30 titles in all, including an Olympic Gold Medal.

The lost and found

1 Find and write the materials hidden in the sentences.

1 They issued eight hundred extra tickets for the concert. *suede*

2 She likes visiting old monuments and museums. _____

3 I don't know where I put that cup last. I can't find it. _____

4 Are we going to the Ascot tonight? _____

5 Jason met Alan three weeks ago. _____

6 I'm tired of urban areas; I'd like to live in the country! _____

2 Match the materials to the pictures and complete the sentences.

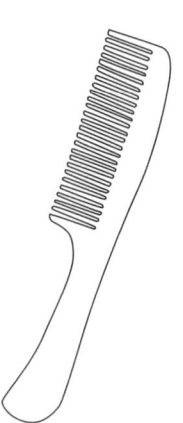

1 The T-shirt is made of _____.

2 The boot is made of _____.

3 The ring is made of _____.

4 The comb is made of _____.

5 The keys are made of _____.

6 The hat is made of _____.

7B Best British Bands

Student A

1 Read the article about the Arctic Monkeys, and fill in the information in the box.

The Arctic Monkeys band was formed in 2002, in Sheffield in the U.K. Their first gig was held in 2003 and their first single was released in May 2005. Their first CD was released in January 2006. Over 350,000 copies of the CD were sold in the first week. They were given the Best British Band award by the NME music magazine in 2006.

	Arctic Monkeys	Kaiser Chiefs
When/formed?	2002	
Where/from?		
First single/released?		
First CD/released?		
How many copies/sold?		
What awards/given? When?		

2 Ask Student B questions about the Kaiser Chiefs, and fill in the information in the box.

A: When were the Kaiser Chiefs formed?   B: In . . .

3 Answer Student B's questions about the Arctic Monkeys.

4 Write three things that the bands have in common.

Both bands _____

_____ .

--- ✂ -

Student B

1 Read the article about the Kaiser Chiefs, and fill in the information in the box.

The Kaiser Chiefs band was formed in 2003 in Leeds in the U.K. Their first gig was held in 2003. Their first single was released in 2004. A year later their first CD, the *Employment*, was released and sold over three million copies. In July 2005 they were asked to play at the "Live 8" concert in London. They were given the Best British Band award at the Brit Awards in 2006.

	Arctic Monkeys	Kaiser Chiefs
When/formed?		2003
Where/from?		
First single/released?		
First CD/released?		
How many copies/sold?		
What awards/given? When?		

2 Answer Student A's questions about the Kaiser Chiefs.

3 Ask Student A questions about the Arctic Monkeys, and fill in the information in the box.

B: When were the Arctic Monkeys formed?   A: In . . .

4 Write three things that the bands have in common.

Both bands _____

_____ .

What's the difference?

Student A

Four pictures in the grid are in the same position as the pictures on Student B's card (e.g., D2).
Ask and answer questions to find out which pictures are in different positions.

A: Let's start with B2. My picture's a bush. What about yours?

B: Mine's a mountain. OK. My turn. D2. My picture's a waterfall.

A: Great. Mine is a waterfall, too.

	A	B	C	D	E
1	house	tree	mountain	flower	sea
2	island	bush	river	waterfall	road

✂ --

Student B

Four pictures in the grid are in the same position as the pictures on Student A's card (e.g., D2) .
Ask and answer questions to find out which pictures are in different positions.

A: Let's start with B2. My picture's a bush. What about yours?

B: Mine's a mountain. OK. My turn. D2. My picture's a waterfall.

A: Great. Mine is a waterfall, too.

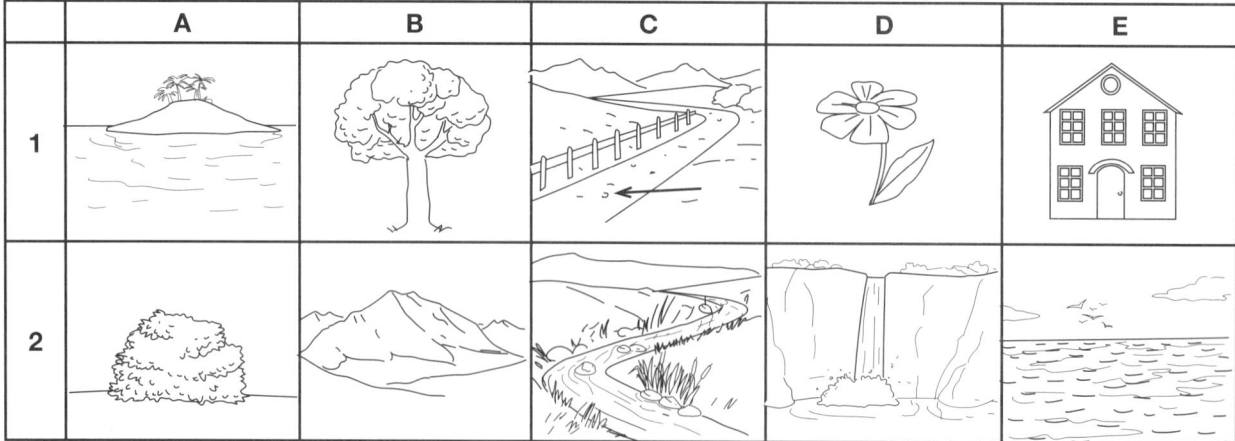

1 **Read the lines from the story and number them in the correct order. Start with A.**

| 1 | A It was Sunday evening. Rachel was alone in the big, old house∧.

                                               e) , where she had lived all her life

☐ B "Kids!" she thought. She was closing the door when she saw a box.

☐ C She stopped reading and looked at the clock.

☐ D It was past midnight. She went to the door and opened it slowly.

☐ E In the box there was a photograph of a child.

| 10 | F She picked up the telephone and dialed the number . . .

☐ G She was reading a book when suddenly somebody knocked at the door.

☐ H She took the box into the kitchen, and opened it.

☐ I The photograph had a telephone number on the back.

☐ J There was no one there! She looked across the street, but couldn't see anyone.

2 **Insert each of the following nonrestrictive relative clauses in an appropriate position in the sentences above. Two of the sentences will not have a nonrestrictive relative clause.**

a) where there were three parked cars
b) which she had almost finished
c) who was strangely familiar
d) which was usually locked

e) ~~, where she had lived all her life~~
f) which wasn't heavy
g) which was ticking loudly
h) which was written in black pen

3 **In less than 30 words, write your own ending to the story.**

_____

_____

_____

_____

Complete the sentences with the correct passive form of the verbs in parentheses. Then write T for *True* or F for *False*.

1 *A Tale of Two Cities* <u>was written</u> (write) by Shakespeare. ☐ F

2 The 2008 Summer Olympics _____ (hold) in Beijing. ☐

3 Coffee _____ (grow) in Africa. ☐

4 Thanksgiving _____ (celebrate) in October in the U.S.A. ☐

5 Mount Everest _____ (climb) by Hillary and Norgay in 1953. ☐

6 The telephone _____ (invent) by Alexander Graham Bell. ☐

7 The World Wide Web _____ (create) in 1999. ☐

8 Chewing gum _____ (make) with petroleum. ☐

9 Many people _____ (drown) by Hurricane Katrina. ☐

10 The *Mona Lisa* _____ (paint) by Michelangelo. ☐

11 John Lennon _____ (murdered) in New York in 1980. ☐

12 Albert Einstein _____ (born) in Austria. ☐

13 The Wimbledon tennis tournament _____ (hold) in Manchester, U.K. ☐

8A Which vacation?

1 Complete the profiles with the correct words or phrases.

Jan is looking for an activity vacation, and she loves the country. She would love to

¹ *go climbing* 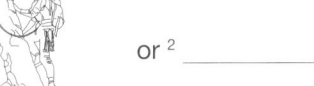 or ² _____.  She likes visiting different countries,

but she doesn't like ³ _____.  She would prefer to find a small hotel.

Sarita has been very busy at work and wants a quiet, relaxing vacation. She loves

⁴ _____,   and ⁵ _____.

Beto and Mona are culture addicts! They've been all over Europe and would like to visit a new city. They

love ⁶ _____.  They always go to museums and ⁷ _____,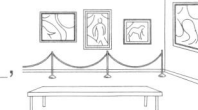

and if they have time they like ⁸ _____,  too!

2 Look at the ads and choose the best vacation for each person.

Jan: Vacation _____   Sarita: Vacation _____   Beto and Mona: Vacation _____

ECOTOURS UNLIMITED
Join us as we camp on the beach in Costa Rica and watch the sea turtles! Airfare and all meals included.

Enjoy the beauty of Baja!
Clean beaches, clear blue sea, peace and quiet. Accommodations near the beach, local food.

WEEKEND CITY BREAKS
We can organize your perfect weekend break . . .
New York, Cairo, Buenos Aires
You choose!
Regular flights and comfortable hotels

Get away from it all . . .
Cottages to rent in the north of Scotland.
Peace and quiet, and beautiful countryside
for hikers.

ACTIVE BREAKS
Book now for vacations in Europe and South America.
Climbing, biking, mountain biking, diving . . .
Choice of accommodations (campsite, apartment, hotel)

8B Negative caterpillar

1 Choose the correct adjective for the prefixes in the caterpillar.

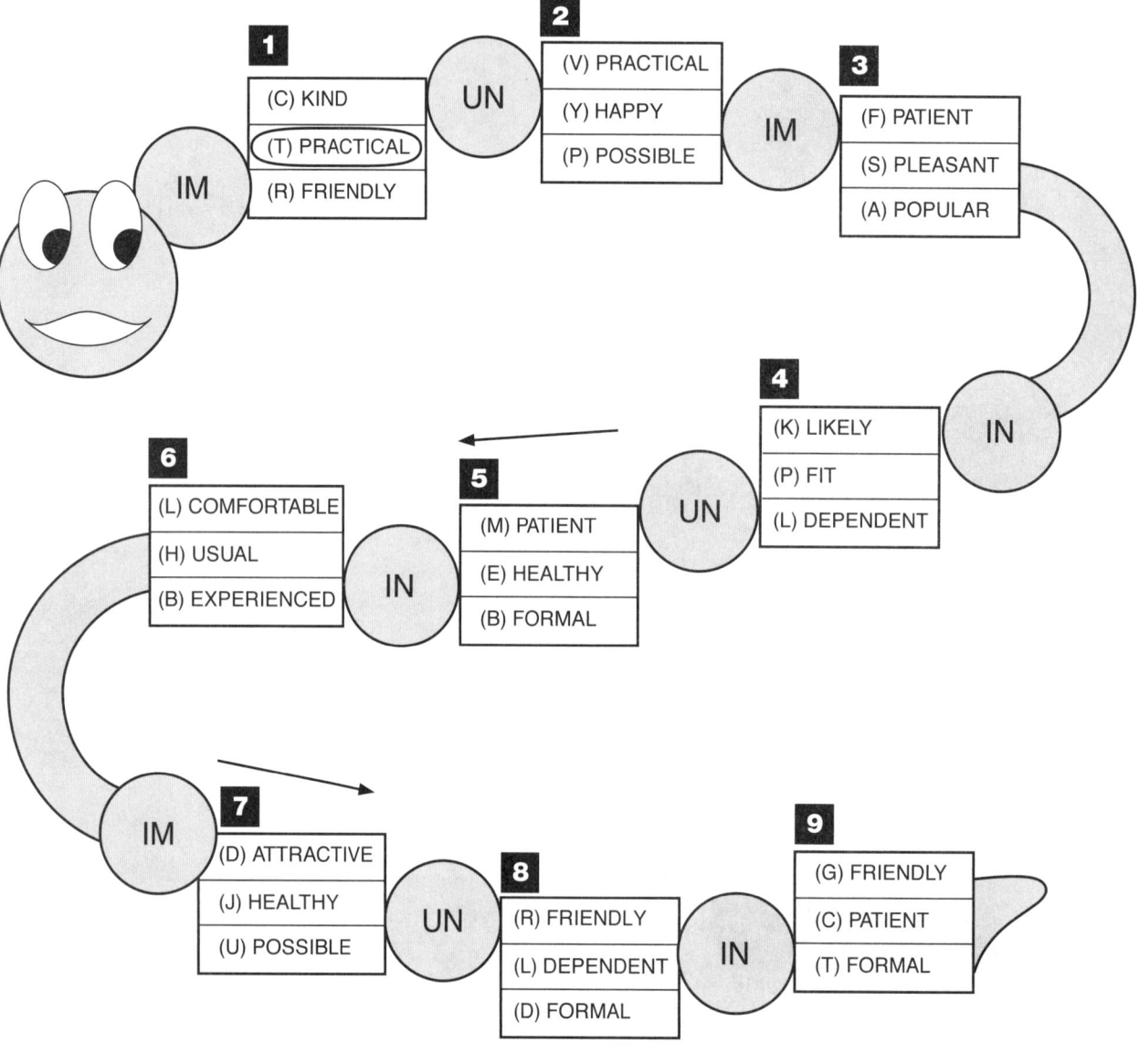

2 Write the letters from the boxes of the correct adjectives: __ __ __ __ __ __ __ __ __

Reorder the letters to finish the sentence: When the caterpillar grows, it becomes a _____.

3 Put the remaining adjectives from Exercise 1 into the correct columns.

IN	IM	UN

8c Going away

Complete the story using the words in the box.

| ~~forget~~ | I'll | it's | want | OK | on | call | promise | remember |
| send | sure | when | will | won't | worry |

1 Don't [1] _forget_ to take your toothbrush.

Don't [2] _____ Mom, I [3] _____.

2 [4] _____ to pack your green shirt. I'll iron it if you [5] _____ me to.

That's [6] _____. I'll do it.

3 Don't forget to [7] _____ me [8] _____ you arrive.

Mom, I [9] _____ I won't forget.

4 Remember, [10] _____ your sister's birthday [11] _____ Sunday!

It's OK, Mom, [12] _____ remember to call her.

5 Make [13] _____ you [14] _____ me an e-mail.

I [15] _____, don't worry.

6 So, where do you need to go?

Uhm . . . Wait a second . . . MOM!!

1 Alice's letter to Maria has been torn up by mistake. Put the pieces in order and write the letter below.

☐ are you? It was great to	☐ Thanks a lot	☐ be cold here, so make

☐ and I had a great time. Thanks

☐ forward to your visit at Christmas. Remember it will

☐ haven't written sooner. How

1 Dear Maria,

☐ you in December.

☐ for everything. Don't

☐ see you in Miami. Sam

☐ all for now, see

☐ for your letter. Sorry I

☐ forget to send us your photos! We're looking

☐ Love, Alice

☐ sure you have summer clothes! Well, that's

2 Alice made a mistake in her letter. Can you find the mistake and correct it?

Story machine: What should she do?

1 Jackie has a problem. Her friends have invited her to a party, but her parents say she can't go because she has a math test tomorrow. Select the correct route through the story machine to understand her problem.

If I ———

1	will go to the party,	go to the party,	won't go to the party,
2	I might not fail the math test.	I can fail the math test.	I might fail the math test.
3	Unless Mom and Dad	If Mom and Dad	Because Mom and Dad
4	find out I lied,	will find out I lied,	won't find out I lied,
5	they'll be really angry.	they won't be really angry.	they are very angry.
6	But if I won't go to the party,	But if I will go to the party,	But if I don't go to the party,
7	my friends won't be upset.	my friends are being upset.	my friends will be upset.
8	So, when I see Mom and Dad	So, when I'm seeing Mom and Dad	So, when I'll see Mom and Dad
9	I told them I'm going to Sally's to study,	I tell them I'm going to Sally's to study,	I'll tell them I'm going to Sally's to study,
10	and if we'll go to the party for an hour (or two)	and if we go to the party for an hour (or two)	and if we won't go to the party for an hour (or two)
11	Mom and Dad will always know . . .	Mom and Dad won't never know . . .	Mom and Dad will never know . . .
12	as soon as my brother Jay	unless my brother Jay	when my brother Jay
13	is at the party . . .	will be at the party . . .	is being at the party . . .

2 Help Jackie decide what to do by writing the possible positive and negative consequences of going to the party.

Positive	Negative
	She might fail her math test.

3 What do you think? Is it a good idea for Jackie to go to the party? Why or why not?

9A Happy birthday!

1 In each bubble, circle the adjective that doesn't belong.

1
metal
cotton
plastic
(white)

2
big
new
small
fat

3
young
leather
old
ancient

4
round
square
expensive
rectangular

5
interesting
Italian
useful
popular

6
little
wool
large
slim

7
fantastic
beautiful
exciting
enormous

8
warm
gold
cotton
suede

2 Complete the sentences below with the circled adjectives from Exercise 1. Then answer these questions. What would Lucky Leo like for his birthday? What is his wife, Busy Bella, going to give him?

1 Lucky Leo would like an _____ _____ _____ sports car

with _____ _____ seats.

2 Busy Bella is going to give him an _____ _____ _____ sweater.

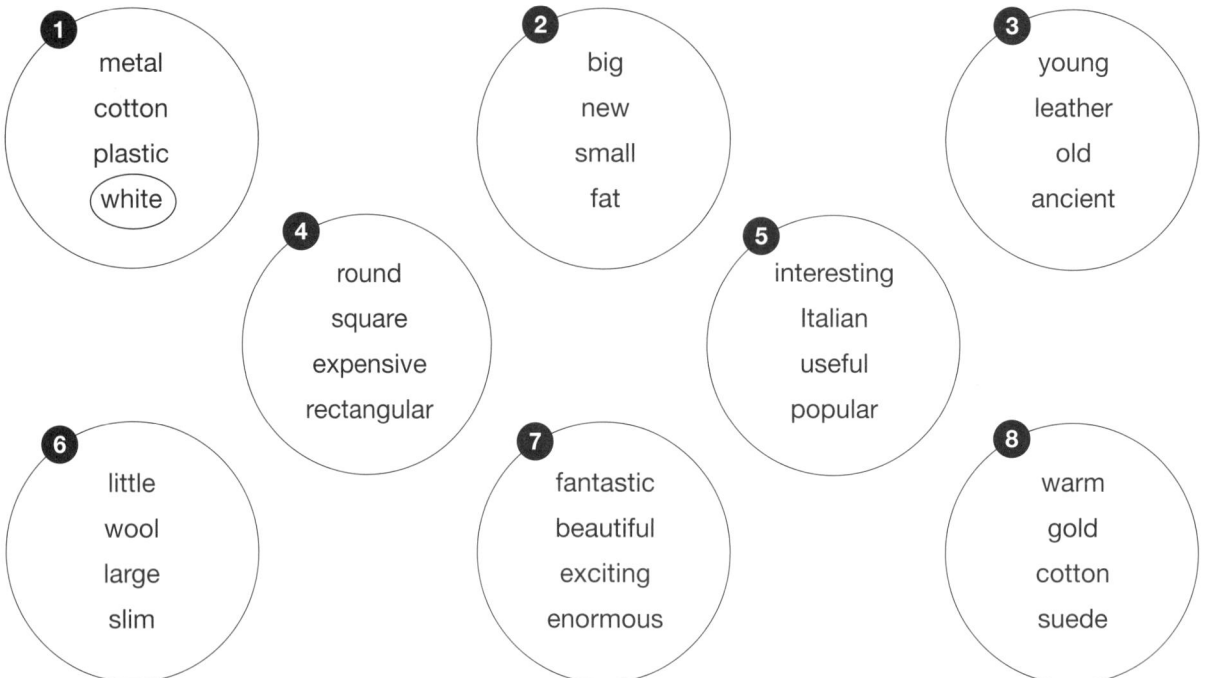

9B Husbands and wives

Read the descriptions and identify the husbands and the wives. Write their names under the pictures and complete the sentences.

1 *Paolo*

2 _____

3 _____

4 _____

5 _____

6 _____

- Paolo's hair is short. He's in his fifties.
- Sanjay's wife has long hair.
- Liz's husband has wavy hair.
- Laura's husband has a beard.
- The well-built man's wife doesn't have a ponytail.
- The well-built man's wife has dark hair and wears eyeglasses.

- Jean often goes to the gym, but she's a bit overweight.
- George is tall, but his wife is the shortest of the three women.
- Sanjay's wife doesn't wear eyeglasses.
- Liz is short.
- Sanjay doesn't wear eyeglasses.

_____ is married to _____.

_____ is married to _____.

_____ is married to _____.

9c A visitor

1 Sam needs help, so he calls his friend Luis. Use the phrases in the box to complete the conversation.

> could you   How are you?   ~~Is Luis there?~~   it's Sam
> get him   What does she look like?   what's her name?
> What time is she arriving?   You're welcome   in her

Woman's voice: Hello?

Sam: Oh hello. ¹ *Is Luis there?*

Woman's voice: Yes, hold on. I'll ² _____.

***

Luis: Hello?

Sam: Oh hi, Luis, ³ _____.

Luis: Hi, Sam. ⁴ _____

Sam: Good, thanks. Luis, ⁵ _____ meet my cousin at the station this afternoon? I have a problem with my car.

Luis: No problem. ⁶ _____

Sam: At three thirty. She'll be on the train from Boston.

Luis: OK. I'll be there. So . . .

Luis: ⁷ _____.

Sam: Oh yeah! Well, she's ⁸ _____ twenties, and she's tall and slim. She usually has her hair in a long ponytail.

Luis: OK. By the way, ⁹ _____?

Sam: Alice. I'll tell her you're coming.

Luis: OK, see you later then.

Sam: Thanks again, Luis.

Luis: ¹⁰ _____. Bye!

Sam: Bye!

2 When Luis arrives at the station, he finds four girls waiting. Which one is Alice? ☐

A

B

C

D

Complete the crossword puzzle using the word and picture clues.

Across

3

He has a _____ on his face.

4

He's got short, _____ hair.

5

She wears her hair in a _____.

7 I'm _____ John's not here at the moment.

9 She needs to go on a diet, she's

_____.

10 He's got no hair. He's completely _____.

Down

1 A person who illegally enters a house and takes things

2 He's not here at the moment. Can I take a _____?

6 "Can I speak to Sally, please?"
"_____ _____, I'll get her."

8 He _____ his head yesterday. Now he has no hair.

A strange conversation

1 **Read Jenny's story about a telephone call. Then complete the telephone conversation between Jenny and her cousin, Tom.**

I had a strange phone call from my cousin Tom yesterday. He asked me what I was going to do for my birthday. I told him I didn't have any plans. Then he asked if I liked dancing. I told him I loved dancing. He asked me if I'd been to that new club, the Ritzy. I said I hadn't, but I'd love to go. Then he asked if I was vegetarian! I said I wasn't. Finally, he asked for your phone number and Sally's number and Daisy's. I gave him the numbers; and then he suddenly said he had to go because he was very busy! It was very strange. Did he call you, Kate?

Tom: *What are you going to do for your birthday?* _____

Jenny: _____

Tom: Do you _____ ?

Jenny: _____

Tom: Have _____ ?

Jenny: _____

Tom: _____ ?

Jenny: _____

Tom: Can you _____ ?

Jenny: Yes, it's 717-555-3417.

Tom: Thanks. I _____

2 **Why did Tom call Jenny and ask her so many questions?**

_____

1 Complete the sentences with the correct adjective. Then write the adjectives in the boxes.

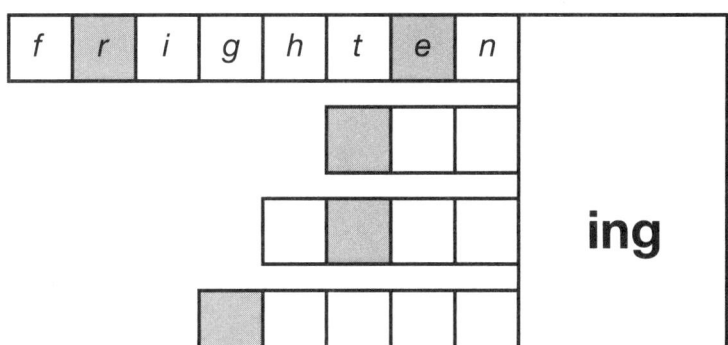

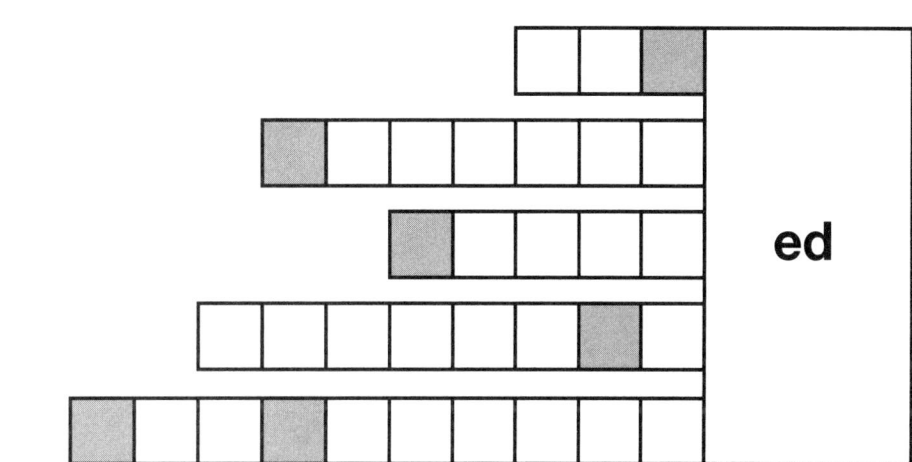

1 I couldn't sleep after that horror movie last night. It was so _f r i g h t e n i n g_.

2 The movie was so _ _ _ _ _ _ that I fell asleep.

3 I'm going to go to bed early tonight. I'm very _ _ _ _ _.

4 I thought he was arriving next week. I was _ _ _ _ _ _ _ _ _ _ when I saw him.

5 It was a great party! There were over 200 people. It was really _ _ _ _ _ _ _ _.

6 I'm going to New York tomorrow. It's my first time—I'm very _ _ _ _ _ _ _ _!

7 She likes reading. She's not really _ _ _ _ _ _ _ _ _ _ _ in sports.

8 I couldn't do my homework yesterday because my brother interrupted me
   every five minutes. He was very _ _ _ _ _ _ _ _ _.

9 Unfortunately she didn't get the job. She was very _ _ _ _ _ _ _ _ _ _ _ _ _.

2 Write the highlighted letters in the boxes below. Then rearrange the letters
to discover how Jess felt when she fell off her chair in class last week!

| e | | | | | | | | | | |

She was _____!

10B Phrasal verbs crossword puzzle

Complete the crossword puzzle. Use phrasal verbs with *out*, *up*, or *on* to replace the words in italics.

Across

1 I never *get out of bed* before nine o'clock in the morning.

3 "Oh no! We have *used all of the* gas. We'll have to stop at a gas station."

5 I need to *discover* where John lives. I want to send him a birthday card.

6 Jake was tired and stopped after an hour. I *continued* and won the race.

Down

1 I've *stopped trying* to learn how to play Sudoku.

2 I *switched* the TV *on*, but as usual the programs were really boring.

4 "*Be careful*! You're going to drop that vase, and it's very expensive."

10c What's on TV?

1 Jack, Matt, Holly, and Lucy have agreed to spend the evening at Jack's house to watch TV and see a movie. Read their preferences and help them decide what to watch.

Channel	7:00	7:30	8:00	8:30	9:00	9:30	10:00	10:30
1	**West Siders** Will Allie marry Jason?	**Seattle ROCKS!** Highlights of this year's music festival	**Who's a winner?** Who will take home a million dollars this week?		**I wanna be a star!** The last eight singers battle to become famous. (Highlights tomorrow at 1 P.M.)			
2	**News, sports, and weather**	**Wimbledon** Tennis highlights	**Pop quiz** Four guests join host Andy Sellar to test their pop knowledge		**Movie:** *Die Hard 2* The ultimate Hollywood action movie			
3	**Rose Street** Fascinating documentary looking at daily life in Boston in the 1930s		**News, Sports, and weather**	**Celebrity Island News** Latest news from the celeb reality show	**Madmen and Dogs** Comedy (repeat)	**Movie:** *The Incredibles* Animated action movie		
4	**The sea below us** David Martinborough presents this documentary on the world's oceans (Repeated Sunday at 4 P.M.)		**Talking to the stars** Special guests include comedian David Kay and musician John Weller. Music from The J Files		**Movie:** *Little Miss Sunshine* Enjoyable comedy that received four Oscar nominations			**Today's Winners** Highlights of today's games

1 Lucy and Holly always watch all the soap operas and refuse to miss an episode.

2 Matt and Jack are big tennis fans.

3 Holly lives 5 miles from Jack's house. The last bus leaves at 10:45 P.M.

4 They all like most types of movies, except for Lucy, who hates violent action movies.

5 They all love music programs, but they hate quiz shows.

6 Jack loves all programs about nature, but his friends never watch documentaries.

7 Lucy and Jack have already seen *The Incredibles*, and Matt has it at home on DVD.

8 Holly occasionally follows the fortunes of the young singers in *I wanna be a star!*

9 Lucy doesn't usually watch reality shows, but her favorite actor is in *Celebrity Island*.

Write your chosen solution in the table below.

7:00	7:30	8:00	8:30	9:00	9:30	10:00	10:30
West Siders							

2 The four friends decide to order pizza, but don't want it to arrive during one of their programs. What is the best time for the pizza to arrive? _____

1 Jake and Andy are arranging to meet tonight. Choose the correct answers to complete the text messages. Watch out! There are some spelling mistakes.

1

Do you wants *to go* to a jazz coincert tonight?

a) to go
b) going
c) we go

2

I'm not _____ jmazz.

a) into
b) like
c) interested

3

_____ go to the smovies.

a) Can we
b) Why don't
c) Let's

4

What mbovie _____ see?

a) do you like
b) do you want to
c) would we

5

_____ the news Harry Potter movie?

a) How about
b) Why don't we
c) I'd like

6

No, _____ not see that.

a) I'd prefer
b) I'd rather
c) now about

7

_____ see thate thriller with Braud Pitt.

a) I'd prefer
b) I'd like
c) I'd rather

8

OK, _____ goodd.

a) look
b) is
c) sounds

9

OK c u there at 9.

2 Find the nine extra letters in the text messages and write them in the boxes below. Then use them to complete the reason why Jake and Andy didn't go to the movies.

| s | | | | | | | | |

Jake | | | | | | the | | | | .

Motivator quiz: How honest are you?

Answer the questions. Check your results and find out how honest you are!

What would you do . . .

1 . . . if you found $50 in the street?
 a) I'd take it to the police.
 b) I'd give it to charity.
 c) I'd keep it.

2 . . . if you knew your best friend was cheating on his/her exams?
 a) I'd tell a teacher.
 b) I'd speak to my friend about it, and try to convince him/her to stop.
 c) I'd do nothing. I'd pretend I hadn't seen it!

3 . . . if you were invited to a party, and your parents had said you couldn't go?
 a) I'd stay home.
 b) I'd try to convince my parents.
 c) I'd tell my parents I was going to study with a friend, and then go to the party.

4 . . . if someone offered to sell you a cell phone that you suspected was stolen?
 a) I'd report it to the police.
 b) I'd think about it, then say no.
 c) I might buy it, depending on the price.

5 . . . if a sales clerk gave you too much change?
 a) I'd tell the assistant and return the extra money.
 b) I'd ask the clerk if he/she thought the change was correct.
 c) I'd keep the money.

6 . . . if you wanted to go to a concert but didn't have enough money?
 a) I'd do chores for my parents to earn the money.
 b) I'd borrow the money from my parents and pay it back later.
 c) I'd borrow the money from my parents, but forget to give it back.

Results
Mostly a)   You are an honest person. But did you really tell the truth?!
Mostly b)   You are honest in most situations, but occasionally you are influenced by less honest people around you.
Mostly c)   You are not always honest! You should change your ways.

11A Missing statues

1 Find the phrases connected with crime in the grid. The words in each phrase are linked. You do not need to use all the words in the grid.

break	into	a	a	house	go
stole	💰	building	vandalize	💰	to
three	commit	mug	robbers	rob	prison
police	a	a	gardens	a	bank
💰	crime	person	write	arrest	a
steal	some	💰	graffiti	statues	criminal
from	money	who	vandalize	property	💰
💰	pay	a	fine	arrest	young

1 *break into a building*   5 _____   9 _____

2 _____   6 _____   10 _____

3 _____   7 _____   11 _____

4 _____   8 _____

2 Reorder the remaining ten words from Exercise 1 to create a headline.

_____ _____ _____ _____ _____

_____ _____ _____ _____ _____

11B Computer world

Student A

1 Ask Student B questions to complete the computer magazine ads.

A: How much do the keyboards cost at PC Universe?   B: $40 each.

CLOSE-OUT SALE

Big reductions on a few remaining computer accessories:
Keyboards $_____
Scanners $_____
Printers $_____

PC Universe, 22 Main Road, Oldham

FREE COMPUTER COURSES

- Beginner course: learn to send and receive e-mails
- Internet course: learn to surf the net and download files
- Web designer course: learn to create a website

For info, visit our website: *www.computaskool.com*

HELP!

I have lost a _____.
It contains _____.
If you find it PLEASE contact me.
Jo Meadows, tel. 516–555–0833
E-mail: _____

FOR SALE

I am selling a brand new laptop with 17-inch screen.
Software and antivirus are included.

Only $650

Contact Ray at 914–555–1442

2 Answer Student B's questions using the information from the ads.

✂ -

Student B

1 Answer Student A's questions using the information from the computer magazine ads.

CLOSE-OUT SALE

Big reductions on a few remaining computer accessories:
Keyboards $40 each
Scanners $50 each
Printers $30 each

PC Universe, 22 Main Road, Oldham

FREE COMPUTER COURSES

- Beginner course: learn to _____ and _____
- Internet course: learn to _____ and _____
- Web designer course: learn to _____

For info, visit our website: *www._____*

HELP!

I have lost a memory stick.
It contains important personal files.
If you find it PLEASE contact me.
Jo Meadows, tel. 516–555–0833
E-mail: birdbrain@yippee.com

FOR SALE

I am selling a brand-new _____ with 17-inch screen.
_____ and _____ are included.

Only $_____

Contact Ray at 914–555–1442

2 Ask Student A questions to complete the ads.

B: What can you learn in the Beginner computer course?   A: You can learn to send and receive e-mails.

53

11c Lost suitcases

1 Simon, Vicky, Lucy, and David are at the airport. Some of the contents of their suitcases have been mixed up. Read the clues and write the initial of the owner next to each item.

1 Simon is a photographer. He always wears casual clothes, and his pants are so baggy he needs a belt.

2 Vicky is worried because she has an important meeting tomorrow, so she urgently needs her good jacket and pants.

3 Lucy recently spent a lot of money on a pair of very expensive sandals.

4 David will be really upset if he's lost his favorite old T-shirt with the logo. Fortunately he left all his checkered shirts at home, so he hasn't lost those!

5 Vicky never wears jeans. She prefers dresses.

6 Simon hopes he'll find his big jacket. He thinks he left some money in one of the jacket's many pockets.

7 Lucy always wears pants or jeans. She hates skirts and dresses.

8 Vicky thinks she might be cold if she can't find her coat.

9 When she gets home, Lucy's boyfriend is going to love the silk tie she bought him as a present.

10 Simon is so embarrassed by his old sneakers that he is going to leave them at the airport.

2 Write a description of the items in each person's suitcase.

1 Simon's suitcase contained _a pair of pants, a jacket,_ _____

2 Lucy's suitcase contained _____ _____

3 David's suitcase contained _____ _____

4 Vicky's suitcase contained _____ _____

1 Read and complete the conversation. Use *so* with an auxillary verb.

1

Hey Mickey, you look happy.

Yeah. I am REALLY happy.

Yeah? Well, so ¹ *do you*!

So ² _____. I have a new girlfriend.

2

Hey, so ³ _____! I met my new girlfriend last week.

So ⁴ _____. I took her to the movies.

3

Wow! So ⁵ _____! And she has a great dog named Max.

Really? So ⁶ _____ Kaz. Gus, where does your girlfriend live?

4

Karen? She doesn't live here in Oakland.

⁷ _____ Kaz. Ummm . . . Gus, what's Karen's phone number?

5

831–555–9384. Why?

Look! This is Kaz's number . . .

2 What is Kaz's telephone number? Write it below.

_ _ _ - _ _ _ - _ _ _ _

1 Look at the headlines and the sentences. The sentences describe four famous robberies. There are three sentences in each story. Match the sentences to the correct headlines.

Ⓐ **Great Dome robbery fails**

Ⓑ *Great Train Robbers caught*

Ⓒ **BOSTON ART THEFT**

Ⓓ **Secret detectives catch art thieves**

1 Two of the gang climbed a ladder and entered the museum through a window. `D`

2 In March 1990, two men wearing police uniforms walked into an art gallery in Boston. ☐

3 Most of the gang were caught and sent to prison for life. One of them escaped from prison in 1965 and went to Brazil. ☐

4 But the police were waiting for them. They had already replaced the diamonds with copies, and they arrested the robbers before they could escape. ☐

5 In 1994, four Norwegians stole Edvard Munch's painting *The Scream* from the Oslo National Museum. ☐

6 The paintings have never been found. ☐

7 Secret detectives offered the robbers £325,000 ($502,261) for the painting, and the robbers were then arrested by the Norwegian police. ☐

8 On August 8, 1963, 15 men stopped the Glasgow to London mail train. ☐

9 They climbed onto the train and stole 120 mail bags that contained £2.6 million ($4 million). ☐

10 The robbers used smoke bombs to break into the room with the diamonds. ☐

11 They left the gallery with 12 famous paintings that were worth $300 million. ☐

12 On Tuesday November 7, 2000, four robbers broke into the Millennium Dome in London, where diamonds worth £350 million ($5.4 million) were kept. ☐

2 Now write the sentences in the correct order to tell the four stories.

A   Great Dome robbery fails

On Tuesday November 7, 2000, . . .

12A Olympic champions

Tom, Kim, Silvia, and Ron have just finished competing in the Olympic Games in Beijing, China. Read the clues and match the people with their country, sports event, and the medals they won.

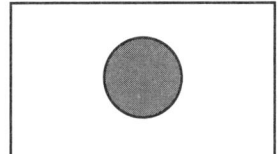
Japan

United Kingdom

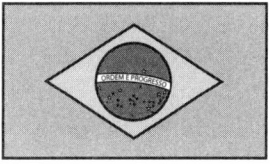
Brazil

U.S.

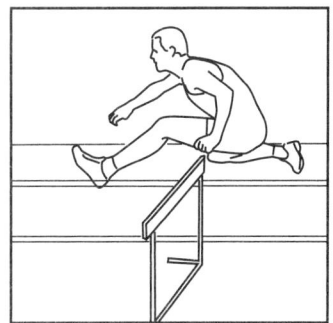

1 Between them, Tom, Kim, Silvia, and Ron won a total of seven medals: three golds, three silvers, and one bronze.
2 Tom is from Europe. He won more medals than Kim, but fewer than Silvia.
3 Kim is from a non-English-speaking country. Her team was very happy to win one silver medal.
4 Silvia won nearly all her races and won three gold medals. Unfortunately, she didn't finish the 100 m race because of a problem with her shoes.
5 Ron always plays his sport with a partner. They were disappointed to lose the final, but happy to win a medal.
6 There were no gold medals for swimming.
7 There was a big welcome-home party in Tokyo for the volleyball team.
8 This country celebrated its new Olympic athletics champion.

Name	Country	Sports event	Medals
Tom	*UK*		
Kim			
Silvia			
Ron			

12B What's the matter?

Student A

1 You are the doctor. Student B will ask you for advice for some problems. Ask how the problem happened or how long he/she has had it. Choose the appropriate treatment from the pictures and give him/her advice.

 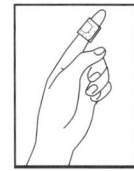 

- Yes, can I help you? . . .
- How did that happen?/How long have you had it?
- Well, if I were you I'd . . .
- I think you should [go straight to the hospital and get an X ray/take some painkillers.

2 You are the patient. You have the following problems. Tell the doctor (Student B) your problem, and ask for help. Answer the doctor's questions.

I've hurt/broken/twisted my . . . [or] I have . . .

 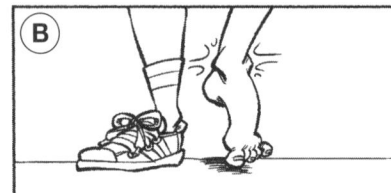 

Student B

1 You are the patient. You have the following problems. Tell the doctor (Student A) your problem, and ask for help. Answer the doctor's questions.

I've hurt/broken/twisted my . . . [or] I have . . .

  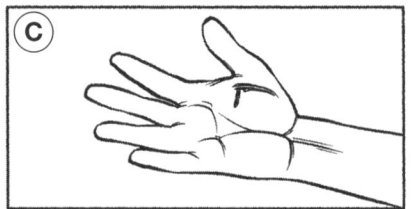

2 You are the doctor. Student A will ask you for advice for some problems. Ask how the problem happened or how long he/she has had it. Choose the appropriate treatment from the pictures and give him/her advice.

 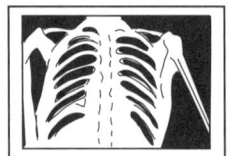 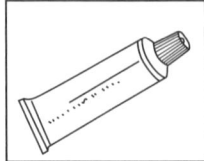

- Yes, can I help you?
- How did that happen?/How long have you had it?
- Well, if I were you I'd . . .
- I think you should [go straight to the hospital and get an X ray/take some painkillers.

12c Adjective honeycomb

Complete the sentences with an adjective and preposition from the grid.
The correct combinations are always next to each other in the grid.

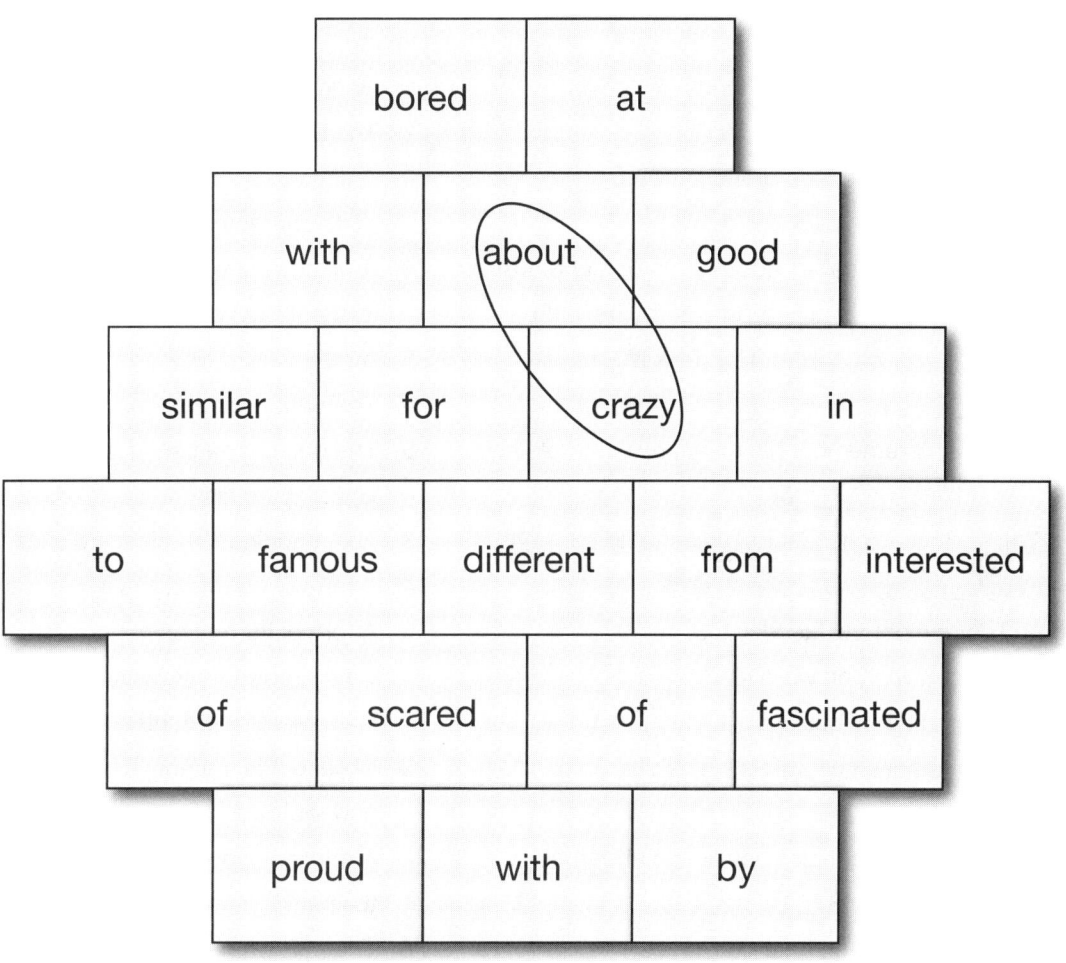

1 I'd rather not go to that restaurant. I'm not _crazy about_ sushi.

2 You passed! Well done, I'm very _____ _____ you.

3 Help! Turn on the light. I'm _____ _____ the dark.

4 Elvis was _____ _____ his acting and his dancing, as well as his singing.

5 She's very _____ _____ her sister. They both have long blond hair and blue eyes.

6 They're very _____ _____ playing cards and want to do something else.

7 I don't think she's _____ _____ going to the museum this weekend.

8 When we visited the wildlife park, I was absolutely _____ _____ the giraffes.

9 It's hard to believe those boys are from the same family. They're so _____ _____ their parents!

12D Consolidation Jumbo crossword puzzle

Complete the crossword puzzle.

Across

1 We wear these on our hands (6)

7 That horror movie was really _____. (5)

9 He ran along the road and jumped _____ the wall. (4)

10 This game is called "football" in England. (6)

11 A sweet food that is produced by bees (5)

12 She's very organized. Her desk is always _____. (4)

15 He can't remember his name, he's completely lost his _____. (6)

16 If you have a headache, you should take a _____. (10)

17 The day before Tuesday (6)

18 Illegal writing on walls (8)

20 A person who cuts hair (11)

23 Your father's new wife's son is your _____. (11)

25 This is what couples usually do after they get engaged. (3, 7)

27 She needs to go on a diet, she's _____. (10)

29 Your mother's brother is your _____. (5)

30 Without hair (4)

31 I'm going to _____ my new shoes to the party. (4)

32 The people who watch a sports event (10)

Down

1 Handsome (4, 7)

2 The Pacific or the Atlantic, for example (5)

3 A fictional TV series that follows the lives of its characters (4, 5)

4 A place where you can read or borrow (but not buy) books (7)

5 Another word for *intelligent* (5)

6 The Sahara or the Gobi, for example (6)

8 The object you use to hit the ball when you play tennis (6)

13 The machine that cleans dishes (10)

14 A term used for sports in general (9)

19 A formal item of clothing that men sometimes wear around their neck (3)

21 The objective of football is to _____ goals! (5)

22 We use this material to make shoes, bags and footballs. (7)

24 A criminal who breaks into houses and steals things (7)

26 The part of the body in the middle of your arm

28 I had a fantastic pizza with sliced tomato and _____ cheese. (6)

Teacher's notes and Answer keys

1A What's your personality?

Aims: To practice adjectives of personality

Instructions: Ex 1 • Give each student a photocopy of the worksheet. • Draw students' attention to the first zodiac profile (Aries) and the first example answer (*sociable*). • Then students rearrange the letters to find the rest of the personality adjectives and complete the profiles.

Ex 2 • Draw students' attention to Sara's date of birth (April 7) and refer back to the profiles to find the zodiac sign (Aries). • Students write the answer on their worksheets, then do the same for the remaining three people.

Ex 3 • Students read the completed profiles from Ex 1, then use the information to decide which person is most compatible with Sara. • Students should use appropriate adjectives to justify their choices.

> **Answer key: Ex 1** 1 sociable 2 friendly 3 easy-going 4 bad-tempered 5 relaxed 6 generous 7 sensitive 8 moody 9 intelligent 10 self-confident 11 shy 12 impatient 13 sensible 14 bossy
> **Ex 2** 1 Aries 2 Sagittarius 3 Gemini 4 Virgo
> **Ex 3** Sara's ideal friend is Alex because he is sensitive and relaxed. (Other answers are also possible.)

1B Where Are You?

Aims: To practice *What/When/Who/Why* questions

Instructions: Ex 1 • Give each student a photocopy of the worksheet. • Ask students if they know what kinds of words are in the box (*question words*). • Explain that students will use the words in the box to fill in the blanks in the instant message.

Ex 2 • Ask students if they know what the numbers to the left of the messages mean. • Explain that this is the time the message was typed. • Before students do the math to answer Ex 2, remind them that there are 60 seconds in a minute.

> **Answer key: Ex 1** 1 Where 2 What 3 When 4 Who 5 Why
> **Ex 2** 36

1C What's my job?

Aims: To practice jobs vocabulary

Instructions: Ex 1 • Give each student a photocopy of the worksheet. • Look at the picture representing 1 Down. • Show students 1 Down in the crossword and point out the number of letters needed (6). Elicit the answer from the students (*farmer*). • Students should write the answer into the crossword and then complete the rest of the crossword.

Ex 2 • Draw students' attention to the highlighted squares in the crossword. • Students should rearrange the letters in the boxes to find the hidden job.

> **Answer key: Ex 1** Across: 4 receptionist 5 builder 7 waitress 9 plumber 11 secretary 12 beautician; Down: 1 farmer 2 actor 3 firefighter 6 electrician 8 nurse 10 dentist
> **Ex 2** designer

1D Consolidation 1 An evening at the movies

Aims: To review question words and question forms

Instructions: Ex 1 • Give each student a photocopy of the worksheet. • Draw students' attention to the question words and phrases in the first box. • Indicate the completed example a) *What time . . . ?* in the second box. • Then students should complete the remaining questions with the words from the first box. • Look at the cartoon pictures and establish that the situation shows two friends talking at the bus stop. • Read the speech bubble in Frame 1 and elicit from the students which question in the box will produce answer d) *Where are you going, Matt?* • Students should complete the cartoon conversation with the questions.

Ex 2 • Students invent a possible answer to the final question h) *Why don't you come?* • Ask students to compare answers in pairs or invite students to share their answers with the rest of the class.

Answer key: Ex 1 1 d) Where are you going, Matt? 2 g) What movie is playing? 3 e) What type of movie is it? 4 c) Who's in it? 5 a) What time does the movie start? 6 f) How long is it? 7 b) How much does it cost? 8 h) Why don't you come?
Ex 2 (possible answer) "I'd love to, but I can't because I'm going to my brother's birthday party."

1D Consolidation 2 Murder at Hogbury Hall

Aims: To review simple past and past continuous

Instructions: Ex 1 • Give each student a photocopy of the worksheet. • Establish the situation for the students and explain any necessary vocabulary: *murder, witness, statement.* • Read Police Officer Plod's notes and ask students questions to check comprehension: "What time did Police Officer Plod arrive?" "Where was the victim?" "What object did he find near the body?" • Look at the first witness statement (Doctor Paul). Read the first sentence, pointing out the example answer for 1. • Ask a student to complete the sentence with the correct form of the verb for 2. • Students should then complete all the witness statements. Check their answers.

Ex 2 • Draw students' attention to the possible methods used to murder the victim, and reread Police Officer Plod's notes. • Draw students' attention to the knife and to the fact that there was no blood. Encourage students to draw logical conclusions from this information (e.g., the knife was not used to murder the victim).
• Organize students into pairs. Point out that one of the witnesses is lying, and that person is the murderer. • Have students read the completed statements and work out the name of the victim, the murderer, and the method, which they write on the worksheet. • Each pair of students joins with another pair to compare answers. • Ask students to give reasons for their answers.

Answer key: Ex 1 1 was walking 2 saw 3 had 4 was making 5 was cleaning 6 heard 7 ran 8 was standing 9 was cleaning 10 was looking for 11 left 12 was washing 13 heard 14 went 15 was running 16 noticed
Ex 2 Victim: Mr. Rogers (his name suggests he is master of the house, he went to the house at 7:20 P.M., there is no witness statement for Mr. Rogers); Murderer: Susie Blue (Dr. Paul saw her at 7:25 P.M., but she says she was washing her hair); Method: poison (Susie Blue was carrying a bottle, there was no blood on the victim)

2A Battle of the Bands

Aims: To practice vocabulary for types of music and musical instruments

Instructions: Ex 1 • Give each student a photocopy of the worksheet. • Draw students' attention to the circled example (*band*), and ask students what the other three words have in common (they are all ways of listening to music). • Students should work in pairs to identify and circle the ones that don't belong. • Check answers with the whole class, and encourage students to justify their answers.

Ex 2 • Students should write the circled words from Ex 1 in the box. • Students should then use the words in the box to complete the interview.

Answer key: Ex 1 1 band 2 gig 3 radio 4 playlist 5 download 6 cello 7 trumpet 8 instrument 9 drums 10 piano
Ex 2 1 band 2 piano 3 instrument 4 drums 5 gig 6 radio 7 download 8 trumpet 9 cello 10 playlist

---

2B What are you doing on Saturday?

Aims: To practice making arrangements, and present continuous for future arrangements

Instructions: • Make a photocopy of the worksheet for each pair of students. • Cut the worksheets in half along the dotted line.
• Organize the students into pairs: Student A and Student B. • Give each student the Student A or Student B section of the worksheet. • Show students that they have a calendar and a poster on their worksheets, and that they are different.

• Explain that students need to arrange to go to each event on the posters at suitable times. • Allow students to work individually to identify suitable times for themselves before they invite their partners to the event on their posters. • Then draw students' attention to the sample conversation. Read the first line of the conversation (A: *Would you like to go to see* The Deep *on Friday evening?*) and elicit the answer from a Student B (*I'm afraid I can't, I'm having pizza with Dave.*). • Repeat this procedure with the second sample conversation. • Students should take turns inviting until they find an appropriate time for each event, which they write in their calendars.

> **Answer key:** *The Deep*: 11 A.M. Sunday   Bowling one-hour game any time on Saturday afternoon

2C Movie reviews

Aims: To practice adjectives of opinion for describing movies, and vocabulary for movie categories

Instructions: Ex 1 • Give each student a photocopy of the worksheet. • Read the first example to students and show them how to complete the adjectives. • Ask students for suggestions of adjectives to complete the first movie review (*fantastic, scary*). • Students should complete the remaining reviews with appropriate adjectives.

Ex 2 • Draw students' attention to the example (1 Nat Coro). • Demonstrate that the name is an anagram of *cartoon*, then refer back to the review and ask students which movie is a cartoon (*The Unbelievables*).
• Students should work out the remaining anagrams and then match the types of movies to the names of the movies in Ex 1.

> **Answer key: Ex 1** 1 amazing 2 fantastic 3 scary
> 4 excellent 5 awesome 6 amusing 7 confusing
> 8 terrible 9 boring 10 sad 11 dull
> **Ex 2** 1 cartoon, *The Unbelievables* 2 western, *Low Morning* 3 horror, *Bad Dreams on Oak Street*
> 4 romantic comedy, *When Larry met Allie*

2D Consolidation 1 Motivator quiz: movies

Aims: To review comparatives and superlatives and movie vocabulary

Instructions: • Give each student a photocopy of the quiz. • Students should answer the quiz questions individually. • Check answers with the whole class. • Students should count up their totals and read their results.

> **Answer key:** 1 b) Robbie Williams 2 b) Danny De Vito
> 3 c) Nicole Kidman 4 b) *Pirates of the Caribbean* (*The Lord of the Rings*, originally a book by J.R.R. Tolkien, *Bridget Jones' Diary*, originally a book by Helen Fielding) 5 c) Robert De Niro (two Oscars: DiCaprio and Bloom currently have no Oscars) 6 b) India
> 7 c) Daniel Radcliffe, star of the Harry Potter movies (b. 1989: King b. 1999, Stewart b. 1990)
> 8 c) *Spiderman 3* ($258 m)

2D Consolidation 2 A busy week!

Aims: To review the present continuous for future arrangements, and making arrangements

Instructions: Ex 1 • Give each student a photocopy of the worksheet. • Draw students' attention to the calendar pages. • Ask students "What is Marcia going to do on Monday?" and elicit the answer, "She's going to meet her agent." • Indicate the example answer given in Frame 1. • Students should look at the cartoon conversation and complete Marcia's answers using the information in the calendar. • Students should reread the completed conversation.

Ex 2 • Elicit from students how they think the man is feeling at the end (unhappy, angry, frustrated?).
• Students should look at the final frame and complete the story.

> **Answer key: Ex 1** 1 I'm meeting my agent
> 2 I'm going to a party 3 I'm playing tennis
> 4 I'm having dinner with the Beckhams
> **Ex 2** 'm sorry / 'd love to, I'm leaving / I'm going away

3A Cleaning up!

Aims: To practice the present perfect simple and *yet/already*

Instructions: Ex 1 • Give each student a photocopy of the worksheet. • Look at the two pictures and ask students what time it is in each picture. • Draw students' attention to the "To Do" list and read the first item on the list (*Do the laundry*). • Draw students' attention to Picture A and the example sentence *Sam hasn't done the laundry yet.* • Then compare with Picture B and the example sentence *He's done the laundry.* • Instruct students to write similar sentences for each item on the "To Do" list.

Ex 2 • Students should look at Picture B and identify the one thing on the "To Do" list that hasn't been done.

> **Answer key: Ex 1** 1 11 A.M. Sam hasn't done the laundry yet. 5 P.M. He's already done the laundry. 2 11 A.M. Sam hasn't cleaned the stove yet. 5 P.M. He's already cleaned the stove. 3 11 A.M. Sam hasn't vacuumed yet. 5 P.M. He's already vacuumed. 4 11 A.M. Sam hasn't done the ironing yet. 5 P.M. He's already done the ironing. 5 11 A.M. Sam hasn't made the bed yet. 5 P.M. He's already made the bed. 6 11 A.M. Sam hasn't emptied the trash yet. 5 P.M. He's already emptied the trash. 7 11 A.M. Sam hasn't washed the dishes yet. 5 P.M. He's already washed the dishes.
> **Ex 2** Sam hasn't fed the cat yet.

3B *Yes!* magazine

Aims: To practice relationships vocabulary and present perfect and simple past

Instructions: Ex 1 • Give each student a photocopy of the worksheet. • Draw students' attention to example answer 1 (*have gotten divorced*) in the article. Ask students why the verb is in the present perfect (recent action in the past with a present result). • Students should complete the rest of the text with verbs from the box, using simple past or present perfect.

Ex 2 • Students should use the completed text from Ex 1 to answer the comprehension questions and find the mystery word in the highlighted letters.

Ex 3&4 • Students should write the mystery word from Ex 2 into the instruction. • Check that students have the correct answer (*third*) before they continue. • Demonstrate to students by counting and circling *year* and then eliciting the next word to circle (*married*). Students should circle every third word. • Students should work in pairs to reorder the circled words to create the mystery fact.

> **Answer key: Ex 1** 1 have gotten divorced 2 have had arguments 3 have broken up 4 made up 5 met 6 asked her out 7 was married 8 was engaged to 9 got engaged 10 got married
> **Ex 2** 1 *True Love* 2 Hollywood 3 wife 4 producer
> **Ex 3&4** Mystery word: third
> Mystery fact: Sixty thousand couples get married in Las Vegas every year.

3C Happy families

Aims: To practice family vocabulary

Instructions: Ex 1 • Give each student a photocopy of the worksheet. • Ask students what relationship Rob and Fiona have with Lillian (son and granddaughter). • Read clue 1 with the students and ask them to identify John (Lillian's husband); then write his name into the family tree. • Students should read the clues and write all the names into the family tree.

Ex 2 • Draw attention to the e-mail signed by "J." • Ask the students which members of the family could have written the e-mail (John, Jeremy, Jean, Julia, Jessica). • Students should read the e-mail and refer to the family tree to identify the writer (Jessica).

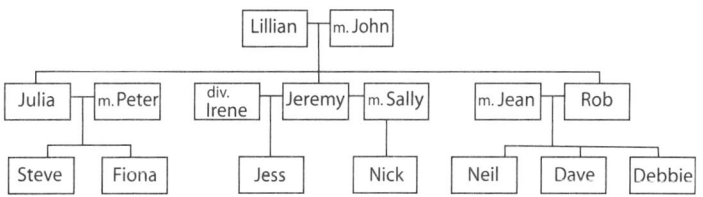

3D Consolidation 1 What's the matter?

Aims: To review present perfect and simple past and talking about problems

Instructions: • Read the first conversation, and ask students for the correct verb forms. • Students should write the verbs in the blanks. • Students should complete conversations 2 and 3. • Students should reread the completed conversations and choose the correct ending for each.

> **Answer key: Ex 1** 1 gotten 2 failed 3 was 4 seen
> 5 looked 6 lost 7 gave 8 taken
> Conversation 1: I've already taken them five times!
> Conversation 2: He was with my girlfriend!
> Conversation 3: I've already looked there. It's disappeared!

3D Consolidation 2 Clauses crossword puzzle

Aims: To review relative clauses and vocabulary from the unit

Instructions: • Give each student a photocopy of the worksheet. • Show students 1 Down on the crossword, and point out the number of letters (5). • Read clue 1 Down and ask students to suggest the answer (*snack*). • Students should write the correct answer in the crossword. • Students should then complete the rest of the crossword.

> **Answer key:** Across: 5 key 6 supermarket 7 stop
> 9 shoe 11 nurse 12 argument; Down: 1 snack
> 2 brother-in-law 3 breakfast 4 head 5 kitchen
> 8 homework 10 wedding

4A A busy day

Aims: To practice vocabulary for places in town

Instructions: Ex 1 • Give each student a photocopy of the worksheet. • Draw students' attention to picture 1 and the example answer. • Look at picture 2 and ask students to suggest the name of the place. • Students should use the pictures to complete the list of places. • Check answers and spelling.

Ex 2 • Draw students' attention to the example answer in Ex 1. Point out the boxed letter and number (7 m). • Then indicate the boxes in Ex 2 and point out the letter *m* in the 7th box. • Students should then write the remaining boxed letters from Ex 1 into the correct box numbers in Ex 2. • Instruct students to complete the sentence with the name of the place they forgot to go to.

> **Answer key: Ex 1** 1 drugstore 2 hospital 3 gas station
> 4 train station 5 supermarket 6 bank 7 library
> **Ex 2** post office / buy stamps

4B Your perfect room

Aims: To practice *too* + adjective, and adjectives and nouns of measurement

Instructions: Ex 1 • Give each student a photocopy of the worksheet. • Read the information and show students the floor plan of the bedroom, pointing out the position of the bed, drawers, door, and window. • Draw students' attention to the description of the first wardrobe. Ask them questions: "How wide is it?" and "How high is it?" Then ask if they think it is OK for the bedroom (Answer: no). Ask students to tell you why not (It's too high). • Students should work in pairs and choose the wardrobe and desk that will fit.

Ex 2 • Draw students' attention to the useful language and give an example for the first wardrobe: "We're not going to buy the Easyfix wardrobe (or stand-alone closet) because it's too high." • Students should prepare justifications for each piece of furniture. • Students should tell the class their choices.

> **Answer key:** The Flatpack wardrobe (along the wall opposite the bed) and the Easydesk (under the window). The Easyfix wardrobe is too high, the Chesterton wardrobe is too wide. The Antique desk is too wide (for the wardrobe): the Spacemaster is too big.

4C The waiting room

Aims: To practice *too much, too many, not enough,* and count and noncount nouns

Instructions: • Give each student a photocopy of the worksheet. • Look at the cartoon story and ask students where the people are (waiting room: doctor or dentist). • Draw students' attention to the example answer in Frame 1. • Students should complete the conversation. • Read the completed conversation as a class.

> **Answer key:** 1 's too much noise 2 's too much pollution 3 's too much traffic 4 are too many people 5 too much money 6 isn't enough respect 7 isn't loud enough

4D Consolidation 1 Can you tell me how to get to . . . ?

Aims: To review asking for and giving directions, and vocabulary for places in town

Instructions: • Make a photocopy of the worksheet for each pair of students. • Cut the worksheet in half along the dotted line. • Arrange the students in pairs. One student in each pair is Student A; the other is Student B.

Ex 1 • Draw students' attention to their task lists. • Ask a Student A to read the first task and ask where he/she needs to go to complete the task. • Repeat this procedure with a Student B. • Students identify where they need to go for each task and write it on their lists.

Ex 2 • Look at the maps with the students and ask them to locate the train station. • Explain that different places are marked on the Student A and Student B maps. • Read the first example question for Student A (*Can you tell me the way to [the post office]?*) and ask a Student B to answer it. • Student As locate the post office and write it onto the map. • Remind students they always start from the station. • Student As ask directions for the places they identified in Ex 1.

Ex 3 • Read the first example question for Student B (*Can you tell me the way to [the library]?*) and ask a Student A to answer it. • Student Bs locate the library and write it onto the map. • Student Bs ask directions for the places they identified in Ex 1. Students compare finished maps to check.

4D Consolidation 2 A trip to New York

Aims: To review transport vocabulary

Instructions: • Give each student a photocopy of the worksheet. • Look at the realia and ask students to look at dates and times to identify which represents the first part of the journey (bus timetable: Headington to Oxford train station).
• Ask students how Jo traveled (by bus).
• Draw students' attention to the example answer.
• Students should number the rest of the details of Jo's trip in order and complete the itinerary with the means of transport or time of the event.

> **Answer key:** 1 Headington to the train station by bus 2 Oxford to London by train 3 Paddington station to Heathrow by subway 4 London to New York by plane 5 JFK Airport to Manhattan by taxi 6 Visit Statue of Liberty by ferry (boat) 7 See Central Park by bike (bicycle) 8 Saturday evening show at 9 P.M. 9 Return home from airport by car with Dave

5A Organized chaos

Aims: To practice collocations with *make* and *do*

Instructions: Ex 1 • Give each student a photocopy of the worksheet. • Read the first sentences of the blog entry and draw students' attention to the example answer for 1. • Ask students to suggest the correct collocation for 2, *make* or *do*, and the correct tense form. • Students should read and complete the rest of the blog entry.

Ex 2 • Students should use the completed blog entry to complete the quiz for Susanna. • Students should count up the responses and read the result.

Ex 3 • Students should answer the quiz questions from Ex 2 for themselves. • Students should count the responses and find their results. • Then students should compare their results in pairs.

> **Answer key: Ex 1** 1 made 2 made 3 do 4 did 5 made 6 made 7 make 8 made
> **Ex 2** 1 a) 2 c) 3 b) 4 c) (mostly c's)

5B The world's most famous spy!

Aims: To practice present perfect continuous with *for* and *since*; to practice asking questions using question words

Instructions: • Make a photocopy of the worksheet for each pair of students. • Cut the worksheets in half along the dotted line. • Give each student a Student A section or a Student B section.

Ex 1 • Ask the first question for Student A, using the prompt (*When did Ian Fleming write the first Bond book?*) and ask a Student B to answer.
• Show Student As where to write the answer.
• Ask the first question for Student B, using the prompt (*How many books have sold since 1952?*) and ask a Student A to answer. • Show Student Bs where to write the answer. • Draw students' attention to the numbering sequence. Then students should ask each other the questions and complete the texts. • When they have finished, students should compare texts to check.

Ex 2 • Draw students' attention to the circled letters in their texts. • Students should write their and their partner's circled letters in the boxes. • Then students should rearrange the letters to answer the question.

> **Answer key: Ex 2** Sean Connery

5C Eating out

Aims: To practice vocabulary for food and cooking

Instructions: Ex 1 • Give each student a photocopy of the worksheet. • Draw students' attention to the example answer in Menu 1. • Students should work out the rest of the anagrams to complete the three menus.

Ex 2 • Look at the pictures of the restaurant signs. • Draw attention to the first sign and ask students to suggest which menu from Ex 1 matches the restaurant and why. • Students should match the remaining signs to the menus. Ask students to justify their answers.

> **Answer key: Ex 1** 1 mushrooms 2 shrimp 3 baked
> 4 mashed 5 vegetables 6 Roast 7 chicken
> 8 Strawberry 9 Sandwiches 10 Burger 11 Grilled
> 12 Tuna 13 fries 14 Garlic 15 salad 16 Chocolate
> 17 Apple 18 Spaghetti 19 lasagna 20 Meat
> 21 cheese 22 pizza
> **Ex 2** A (Menu 3) B (Menu 1) C (Menu 2)

5D Consolidation 1 A birthday celebration

Aims: To review vocabulary for food and cooking

Instructions: Ex 1 • Give each student a photocopy of the worksheet. • Look at the restaurant bill and draw students' attention to the example answer under *Ellie*. • Read the second clue (*Ellie doesn't eat fish or meat*), and indicate the four main courses on the bill to show that Ellie must have had *vegetable pasta*. • Students should work in pairs, read the clues, and use the bill to work out what each person ate. • Students should write the food under each person's name.

Ex 2 • Students should use their answers to Ex 1 and the bill to work out how much each person spent.

> **Answer key: Ex 1** Jessie: onion soup, steak and mashed potatoes, roasted vegetables, chocolate cheesecake; Andy: salmon with roasted potatoes, mixed salad, fruit salad; Ray: shrimp cocktail, roast beef, green salad, apple pie; Ellie: stuffed mushrooms, vegetable pasta, green salad, apple pie
> **Ex 2** Jessie: $24; Ray: $26.25; Ellie: $24.25; Andy: $19.95

5D Consolidation 2 A quiet evening at home

Aims: To review phrasal verbs with *look*

Instructions: • Give each student a photocopy of the worksheet. • Look at the cartoon pictures and establish the situation. Ask students, "What is the relationship between the woman and the boy?" (grandmother and grandson), "Where is the boy's mother?" (probably at work). • Students should look at the pictures and match them to conversations. • Then students complete the conversations with the correct phrasal verb from the box.

6A Rags to riches

Aims: To practice *used to* for describing past habits

Instructions: Ex 1 • Give each student a photocopy of the worksheet. • Draw students' attention to the pictures and the thought bubbles. Establish the situation: a rich man who in the past was very poor. • Focus on the example answer for number 1 in the text (*used to be*) and indicate the verbs in the box. • Do number 2 together: ask students to look at the pictures and choose the correct verb. Remind them they may need to use the negative form of *used to*. • Students then complete the text.

Ex 2 • Draw students' attention to the example answer. Show them the word *But* in the text and the word *millionaire* that precedes it. • Students should find the words in the text and write the preceding words in the spaces. • Students should use the words to complete the headline.

6B Modern-day hero

Aims: To practice verbs of action

Instructions: Ex 1 • Give each student a photocopy of the worksheet. • Draw students' attention to the completed example 5, pointing out the collocation with *over* and *garden wall*, and indicating the verbs in the box. • Students should use the rest of the verbs in the box in the simple past to complete the remaining sentences.

Ex 2 • Focus on the first picture and ask students which sentence from Ex 1 describes the picture (sentence 5). Show students the number 5 in

the corner of the picture box. • Students should match the rest of the sentences to the pictures to complete the story.

6C Mixed-up stories

Aims: To practice the use of narrative tenses: simple past perfect, simple past, and past continuous

Instructions: • Give each student a photocopy of the worksheet. • Read the example sentence A1 and explain this is the first sentence of story A. • Ask students to find the first sentence of story B and write the sentence under the headline. • Then students should identify sentences for story A and story B and put them in the correct order. • Students should write the completed stories under the correct headlines.

6D Consolidation 1 Crossword puzzle

Aims: To review verbs of action and collocations with *lose*

Instructions: Ex 1 • Give each student a photocopy of the worksheet. • Draw students' attention to the clue for 1 Across, and ask them to locate 1 Across on the crossword. • Point out the number of letters (3), and ask students to suggest words. Students write the correct answer in the crossword. • Then students should complete the rest of the crossword.

6D Consolidation 2 Grand Slam Champion!

Aims: To review *used to* and past ability

Instructions: • Make a photocopy of the worksheet for each pair of students. • Cut the worksheets in half along the dotted line. • Organize the students in pairs. One student in each pair is Student A, the other is Student B. • Show students that there is information about Rafael Nadal on the worksheets. • Make the first example question for Student A, using the prompt *when?* (*When was he born?*) and ask a Student B to answer it (*June 3, 1986*). Show students the first example on the worksheet. • Make the first example question for Student B, using the prompt *where?* (*Where was he born?*) and ask a Student A to answer it (*Mallorca, Spain*). Show students the first example on the worksheet. • The students should take turns to ask and answer the questions in pairs, and write the information on their worksheets. • Students should compare their completed worksheets to check their answers.

7A The lost and found

Aims: To practice materials vocabulary

Instructions: Ex 1 • Give each student a photocopy of the worksheet. • Draw students' attention to the example in sentence 1. • Explain that students have to find the hidden word in each sentence. • Students should find the hidden materials and write them next to each sentence.

Ex 2 • Students should match the materials from Ex 1 with the objects in the pictures. Then students should complete the sentences.

7B Best British Bands

Aims: To practice past simple passive

Instructions: • Make a photocopy of the worksheet for each pair of students. • Cut the worksheet in half along the dotted line. • Organize the students into pairs. • Give each student a Student A section or a Student B section.

Ex 1 • Explain that students have information about either the Arctic Monkeys or the Kaiser Chiefs on their worksheets. • Draw students' attention to the prompt questions in the information table. • Students should read the information and complete the column for their bands.

Ex 2&3 • Read the first example question for Student A (*When were the Kaiser Chiefs formed?*) and ask a Student B to answer it (*In 2003*). Show the students where to write the information on the worksheet. • Read the first example question for Student B (*When were the Arctic Monkeys formed?*) and ask a Student A to answer it (*In 2002*). Show the students where to write the information on the worksheet. • The students should take turns asking and answering the questions in pairs and write the information on their worksheets.

Ex 4 • Students should compare the information about the two bands and write three things the bands have in common.

7C What's the difference?

Aims: To practice landscape and environment vocabulary

Instructions: • Make a photocopy of the worksheet for each pair of students. • Cut the worksheets in half along the dotted line. • Arrange the students in pairs and give each student a Student A section or a Student B section. • Show students that they each have a grid with the same pictures, but with some in different positions. • Ask students to find B2 on their grid. • Ask a Student A the first example question (*Let's start with B2, etc.*) and elicit the response (*a bush*). • Ask a Student B (*What about yours?*) and elicit the response (*a mountain*). • Tell students to note the difference by circling the object in C1 (Student A) and B2 (Student B). • The students take turns to ask and answer and find the eight differences in their grids, circling the differences and putting Xs through the pictures that are the same.

> **Answer key:** The different pictures are: A1, C1, E1, A2, B2, E2

7D Consolidation 1 Mystery story

Aims: To review nonrestrictive relative clauses

Instructions: Ex 1 • Give each student a photocopy of the worksheet. • Draw students' attention to the first example sentence. • Explain that this is the first sentence of the story. Point out that sentence F is the last sentence. • Ask the students to read the remaining sentences and suggest the second sentence. • Have students then put the rest of the sentences in the correct order.

Ex 2 • Explain that the sentences in Ex 2 provide more information to add to the story. • Draw students' attention to clause e) and show where it has been inserted into the sentence A1 in Ex 1.
• Point out there are ten sentences in Ex 1 and only eight clauses. Encourage students to find the BEST place for the clause; it is not necessary for every sentence to have a clause. • The students rewrite the sentences from Ex 1 with the added clauses.

Ex 3 • If there is time, ask students to write out the full story so far, in the correct order and with the added clauses. • Students then invent the end of the story in less than 30 words.

> **Answer key: Ex 1** 1 A 2 G 3 C 4 D 5 J 6 B 7 H 8 E 9 I 10 F
> **Ex 2** . . . Rachel was alone in the big, old house **e) , where she had lived all her life.** She was reading a book, **b) which she had almost finished,** when suddenly . . . She stopped reading and looked at the clock, **g) which was ticking loudly.** . . . She went to the door, **d) which was usually locked,** and . . . She looked across the street, **a) where there were three parked cars,** but couldn't . . . "Kids!" she thought. She was closing the door when she saw a box. She took the box, **f) which wasn't heavy,** into the kitchen . . . In the box there was a photograph of a child, **c) who was strangely familiar.** The photograph had a telephone number on the back, **h) which was written in black pen.** (OR The photograph had a telephone number, **h) which was written in black pen,** on the back.) She picked up the telephone . . .

7D Consolidation 2 Motivator quiz: general knowledge

Aims: To review passive forms

Instructions: • Give each student a photocopy of the worksheet. • Draw students' attention to the example answer. • Have students complete the statements in the passive form using the verbs in brackets. • Have them read the completed sentences and decide if they are true or false.
• To add a competitive element to the quiz, arrange the class into teams of three or four and give a time limit to answer the questions.

> **Answer key:** 1 was written (F: Charles Dickens) 2 were held (T) 3 is grown (T: mostly in Northeast and East Africa) 4 is celebrated (F: November) 5 was climbed (T) 6 was invented (F: Meucci, but he didn't request the patent in time, so it is credited to Bell) 7 was created (F: 1989) 8 is made (T) 9 were drowned (T) 10 was painted (F: Leonardo da Vinci) II was murdered (T) 12 was born (F: Germany) 13 is held (F: Wimbledon)

8A Which vacation holiday?

Aims: To practice vocabulary for vacation activities

Instructions: Ex 1 • Give each student a photocopy of the worksheet. • Draw students' attention to the picture and example answer for 1 (*go climbing*). • Ask students to suggest the answer for 2, using the picture clue. • Students then use the pictures to complete the rest of the profiles.

Ex 2 • Read the first complete profile (Jane) together. • Focus on the first ad (A). Ask students if they think it is the best vacation for Jan and why or why not. • Have students read the rest of the ads and choose the best vacation for each person.

> **Answer key: Ex 1** 1 go climbing 2 (go) (mountain) biking 3 (going) camping 4 reading 5 sunbathing 6 sightseeing 7 (art) galleries 9 (going) shopping
> **Ex 2** Jan: Vacation E Sarita: Vacation C Beto and Mona: Vacation B

8B Negative caterpillar

Aims: To practice negative adjectives with prefixes *un-, in-, im-*

Instructions: Ex 1 • Give each student a photocopy of the worksheet. • Focus on the caterpillar and show students the direction in which they need to read the adjectives, starting from the head and ending at the tail. • Draw students' attention to the circled example and establish that *practical* is the only adjective that takes the prefix *im-*. • Students work along the caterpillar and circle the correct adjective for each prefix.

Ex 2 • Focus on the example in Ex 1. Draw attention to the letter in the box of the circled adjective (T). • Show students where to write the letter *T* in the space below the caterpillar. • Have students write the rest of the letters in the spaces. • Students then rearrange the letters to make the word that completes the sentence.

Ex 3 • Focus on the example in Exercise 1. Ask students which prefix they need to make the negative of the two remaining adjectives (*unkind, unfriendly*). • Indicate the three columns and tell

students to write the two adjectives in the correct column. • Students write the rest of the adjectives from the caterpillar in the table.

> **Answer key: Ex 1** 1 impractical 2 unhappy 3 impatient 4 independent 5 unhealthy 6 inexperienced 7 impossible 8 unfriendly 9 informal
> **Ex 2** butterfly
> **Ex 3** IN dependent, formal, IM patient, practical, possible, UN friendly, attractive, comfortable, usual, healthy, likely, fit, pleasant, popular, kind

8C Going away

Aims: To practice reminders, promises/reassurances, and offers

Instructions: • Give each student a photocopy of the worksheet. • Focus on the first frame of the story. Establish the relationship between the two people (mother and son), and the situation (son preparing to go on vacation). • Look at the first blank in the conversation and ask students to suggest which word from the box fits. Students write the word in the blank. • Have students look at the pictures and use the words in the box to complete the rest of the conversation.

> **Answer key:** 1 forget 2 worry 3 won't 4 Remember 5 want 6 OK 7 call 8 when 9 promise 10 it's 11 on 12 I'll 13 sure 14 send 15 will

8D Consolidation 1 A thank-you letter

Aims: To review phrases used in informal letters and reminders

Instructions: Ex 1 • Give each student a photocopy of the worksheet. • Draw attention to example box 1. • Ask students to identify which piece of the letter follows. Students write *2* in the box. • Students then number the rest of the pieces in the correct order. • Show students where to write the correctly ordered letter.

Ex 2 • Have students reread the completed letter and correct the mistake.

8D Consolidation 2 Story machine: What should she do?

Aims: To review first conditional with *if/unless*

Instructions: Ex 1 • Give each student a photocopy of the worksheet. • Draw students' attention to the example in line 1. • Ask students to suggest the correct sentence in line 2. • Have students draw a line to connect the correct sentences in lines 1 and 2. • Students continue the "story" and choose the correct sentence on each line.

Ex 2 • Have students read through the completed problem in Exercise 1. • They then identify all the consequences of going to the party and write them in the positive or negative column.

Ex 3 • Tell students to use the chart of consequences to decide if it is a good idea for Jackie to go to the party. • Have them share their ideas with the class.

Answer key: Ex 1 1 go to the party 2 I might fail the math test. 3 If Mom and Dad 4 find out I lied 5 they'll be really angry. 6 But if I don't go to the party, 7 my friends will be upset. 8 So, when I see Mom and Dad 9 I'll tell them I'm going to Sally's to study, 10 and if we go to the party for an hour (or two) 11 Mom and Dad will never know . . . 12 unless my brother Jay 13 is at the party. . . .
Ex 2 Positive consequences: her friends will be happy, she'll enjoy herself **Negative consequences:** she may fail her math test, she'll have to lie to her parents, her brother might be there, her parents may find and out and they'll be very angry
Ex 3 No: the negative consequences easily outweigh the positive.

9A Happy birthday!

Aims: To practice adjective word order

Instructions: Ex 1 • Give each student a photocopy of the worksheet. • Draw students' attention to the example in bubble 1 and ask the students why *white* is the adjective that doesn't belong (it's a color; the others describe materials). • Students then circle the adjective that doesn't belong in each of the rest of the bubbles. • Ask students to justify their answers.

Ex 2 • Focus on the pictures and identify the object Lucky Leo would like (a sports car) and the object his wife is going to give him (a sweater). • Ask students to suggest which of the adjectives they circled in Ex 1 could be used with the car and which with the sweater. • Have students complete the descriptions with the adjectives from Exercise 1, putting them in the correct order.

Answer key: Ex 1 1 white 2 new 3 leather 4 expensive 5 Italian 6 wool 7 enormous 8 warm
Ex 2 1 Lucky Leo would like an expensive, new, Italian sports car with white leather seats. 2 Busy Bella is going to give him an enormous, warm wool sweater.

9B Husbands and wives

Aims: To practice appearance vocabulary

Instructions: • Give each student a photocopy of the worksheet. • Draw students' attention to the picture of Paolo. • Read the first clue. Indicate why this picture must be Paolo (he has short hair and is the oldest of the three men). • Read the second clue and ask students to point at the woman this logically eliminates. • Have students work in pairs and use the clues to work out the names of each person and who is married to whom.

Answer key: 1 Paolo 2 George 3 Sanjay 4 Jean 5 Laura 6 Liz
Paolo is married to Laura, George is married to Liz, Sanjay is married to Jean

9C A visitor

Aims: To practice the language of telephone conversations and review appearance vocabulary

Instructions: Ex 1 • Give each student a photocopy of the worksheet. • Draw students' attention to the first part of the conversation and the example answer. • Students then complete the rest of the conversation with phrases from the box.

Ex 2 • Draw students' attention to the pictures of the four girls. • Have students read the description in the conversation from Exercise 1 and circle *Alice*.

> **Answer key: Ex 1** 1 Is Luis there? 2 get him
> 3 it's Sam 4 How are you? 5 could you 6 What time is
> she arriving? 7 What does she look like? 8 in her
> 9 what's her name? 10 You're welcome
> **Ex 2** B

9D Consolidation 1 Crossword puzzle

Aims: To review vocabulary from the unit

Instructions: • Give each student a copy of the worksheet. • Draw students' attention to the picture clue for 4 Across. • Ask students to locate 4 Across on the crossword and establish the number of letters (six). • Ask students to suggest the answer, and then write the correct answer onto the crossword. • Have students read the rest of the clues and complete the crossword.

> **Answer key:** Across: 3 scar 4 spiky 5 ponytail
> 7 afraid 9 overweight 10 bald
> Down: 1 burglar 2 message 6 Hang on 8 shaved

9D Consolidation 2 A strange conversation

Aims: To review reported statements and reported questions

Instructions: Ex 1 • Give each student a photocopy of the worksheet. • Tell students to read the story

in the speech bubble. • Ask students some simple comprehension questions: "Who called Jenny yesterday?" (Her cousin Tom), "Who is she talking to now?" (Kate), "Whose phone number did he ask for?" (Kate's), "Whose birthday is it soon?" (Jenny's). • Draw students' attention to the first line of the conversation. Ask students to identify the equivalent part of the conversation in the speech bubble. • Ask students to give Jenny's response and write it in the space. • The students then use Jenny's story to complete the conversation.

Ex 2 • Tell students to discuss the question in pairs and report back to the class.

> **Answer key: Ex 1** Tom: What are you going to do for
> your birthday? Jenny: I don't have any plans. Tom: Do
> you like dancing? Jenny: I love dancing. Tom: Have
> you been to that new club, the Ritzy? Jenny: No, I
> haven't, but I'd love to go. Tom: Are you vegetarian?
> Jenny: No, I'm not. Tom: Can you give me Kate's
> phone number? Jenny: Yes, it's 717–555–3417.
> Tom: Thanks. I have to go, I'm very busy!
> **Ex 2** He is planning a birthday surprise for Jenny.

10A How did she feel?

Aims: To practice *-ed* and *-ing* adjectives

Instructions: Ex 1 • Give each student a photocopy of the worksheet. • Draw students' attention to the first clue and example answer. • Show students where to write the answers for *-ed* or *-ing* adjectives in the boxes. (The order of the boxes corresponds to the order of the clues.) • Have students read and complete the sentences, then write the correct adjectives in the boxes.

Ex 2 • Draw students' attention to the highlighted letters in the boxes in Ex 1. • Students write the highlighted letters in the boxes in Ex 2. • Have students rearrange the letters to find another adjective to complete the sentence.

> **Answer key: Ex 1** 1 frightening 2 boring 3 tired
> 4 surprised 5 amazing 6 excited 7 interested
> 8 annoying 9 disappointed
> **Ex 2** embarrassed

10B Phrasal verbs crossword puzzle

Aims: To practice phrasal verbs with *out, up, on*

Instructions: • Read the clue for 1 Across. • Tell students to locate 1 Across on the crossword and establish the number of letters (5). Remind students the answer is a phrasal verb, so it is made of at least two words. • Ask students to suggest possible answers, then write the answer onto the crossword. • Remind students the verbs must be in the correct tense to complete the clues. Students then complete the rest of the crossword.

> **Answer key:** Across: 1 get up 3 run out of 5 find out
> 6 went on;
> Down: 1 given up 2 turned on 4 look out

10C What's on TV?

Aims: To practice vocabulary for types of TV programs

Instructions: Ex 1 • Give each student a photocopy of the worksheet. • Read the first clue. Ask students to identify a program on the timetable that Lucy and Holly will want to watch (*West, Siders* Channel 1). • Have students work in pairs and read all the clues to choose the best programs for the friends to watch. Show students where to write their solution.

Ex 2 • Tell students use their solution and the clues in Exercise 1 to decide the best time for the pizza to arrive.

> **Answer key: Ex 1** 1 7:00 West Siders; 7:30 Seattle
> ROCKS; 8:30 Celebrity Island; 9:00 Little Miss
> Sunshine; 10:30 Today's Winners
> **Ex 2** 8–8:30.

10D Consolidation 1 An invitation

Aims: To review making suggestions and expressing preferences

Instructions: Ex 1 • Give each student a photocopy of the worksheet. • Focus on the first

text message. Point out that there are some spelling mistakes in the message (e.g., *want, concert*). • Have students read the rest of the text messages and choose correct answers to fill the blanks.

Ex 2 • Draw attention again to the spelling mistakes in the first text message. • Ask students to identify the extra letters in the words *want* and *concert* (*s* and *i*). • Tell students to write the extra letters in the boxes. • Tell students to find and write the rest of the extra letters from the text messages. • They rearrange the letters to make the two words to complete the sentence.

> **Answer key: Ex 1** 1 a) 2 a) 3 c) 4 b) 5 a) 6 b) 7 c) 8 c)
> **Ex 2** Jake missed the bus.

10D Consolidation 2 Motivator quiz: How honest are you?

Aims: To review second conditional

Instructions: • Give each student a photocopy of the quiz. • Students work individually to answer the questions. • Students count up their answers and read the analysis. • Have them compare their answers with a partner and say if they agree with the analysis.

11A Missing statues

Aims: To practice crime vocabulary

Instructions: Ex 1 • Give each student a photocopy of the worksheet. • Draw students' attention to the example answer (*break into a building*). • Ask students to find and circle the phrase in the chart. • Point out that the words in each phrase are always next to each other in the chart. Tell students that not all words in the chart are needed. • Tell students to find and circle the rest of the eleven phrases connected with crime in the chart and complete the list.

Ex 2 • Tell students to find the remaining ten words in the chart. • They rearrange the words to create the newspaper headline.

11B Computer world

Aims: To practice computer language

Instructions: • Make a photocopy of the worksheet for each pair of students. • Cut the worksheets in half along the dotted line. • Arrange the students in pairs. One student in each pair is Student A, the other is Student B.

Ex 1&2 • Show the students the four ads and the information they need to complete. • Ask the example question for Student A (*How much do the keyboards cost at PC Universe?*) and ask a Student B to answer. Show the students where to write the information on their worksheets. • Ask the example question for Student B (*What can you learn in the Beginner computer course?*) and ask a Student A to answer. Show the students where to write the information on their worksheets. • Tell students to take turns to ask and answer the questions in pairs and write the information on their worksheets.

11C Lost suitcases

Aims: To practice vocabulary for clothes, accessories, styles, and patterns

Instructions: Ex 1 • Read the first clue to the students. Ask students to identify the picture of the baggy pants with belt on the worksheet. • Explain that the clues tells us that the baggy pants are Simon's, so there is an "S" in the box to indicate *Simon*. • The students read the other clues, identify who the clothes belong to, and write the initial for each item. • Help students, if necessary, to workout who the checked shirt belongs to.

Ex 2 • Show students the example description of Simon's suitcase. • Ask students then what other items were in Simon's suitcase (a pair of sneakers and a checked shirt), and show them where to add this information. • Tell students to write similar descriptions of the other three suitcases, using the information from Exercise 1.

11D Consolidation 1 Whose girlfriend?

Aims: To review positive and negative echo answers

Instructions: Ex 1 • Draw students' attention to the first frame of the story. • Read the first two lines of the conversation, pointing out the example echo answer. • Read the second two lines of the conversation and elicit the echo answer for number 2. Students should write the correct echo answer in the space. • Then students should complete the rest of the conversation.

Ex 2 • Have students read the full conversation. • Students should discuss why Mickey shows Gus Kaz's number, and why Gus is shocked (because Karen and Kaz are the same person). • Students should write Kaz's (Karen's) telephone number in the space.

11D Consolidation 2 Famous robberies

Aims: To review crime vocabulary

Instructions: Ex 1 • Give each student a photocopy of the worksheet. • Read the four headlines to the students. • Draw students' attention to the first sentence and explain that the example letter in the box refers to headline D. • Ask students to read all the sentences and to identify two more sentences that refer to headline D (5 and 7) • It is important that students read all the clues in order to do the exercise. Suggest to students that they identify the first line of each story FIRST, as they give the clues to the following lines. Then tell them to look out for words that link clues (e.g., *museum* and *Norwegian*). • Students should work in pairs to identify which lines go with which headline.

Ex 2 • Read the example to the students. • Ask them to tell you the rest of the story in a logical order. • Then students should write each of the stories in the correct order, starting with the appropriate headline.

> **Answer key: Ex 1** 1 D 2 C 3 B 4 A 5 D 6 C 7 D
> 8 B 9 B 10 A 11 C 12 A
> **Ex 2:** (correct order) A 12, 10, 4   B 8, 9, 3
> C 2, 11, 6   D 5, 1, 7

12A Olympic champions

Aims: To practice sport vocabulary

Instructions: • Give each student a photocopy of the worksheet. • Show students the national flags and then ask them to name the sports represented by the pictures (volleyball, athletics, swimming, tennis). • Draw students' attention to the table at the bottom of the worksheet and the example answer. • Point out to students the reason for this answer: Tom must be from the UK, because it is the only one of the four countries in Europe. • Have students read the clues and complete the table.

> **Answer key:** Tom: UK, swimming, 2 medals (1 silver, 1 bronze) Kim: Japan, volleyball, 1 medal (silver) Silvia: Brazil, athletics, 3 medals (gold) Ron: U.S. tennis, 1 medal (silver)

12B What's the matter?

Aims: To practice asking for and giving advice, and vocabulary for injuries and medical treatment

Instructions: Ex 1&2 • Make a photocopy of the worksheet for each pair of students. • Cut the worksheets in half along the dotted line. • Organize students into pairs. One student in each pair is Student A, the other is Student B. • Give each student a Student A section or a Student B section. • Show students the pictures that represent a health problem they need advice for, and the pictures that represent advice for each others' problems. • Read the first example situation for Student B (*I've hurt my arm*). • Student As look at their pictures and respond with appropriate advice. (*If I were you, I'd go to the hospital; You should have an X ray*). • Read the first example situation for Student A (*I've got a temperature and a headache*). • Student Bs look at their pictures and respond with appropriate advice. (*If I were you, I'd go to bed and take some painkillers*). • Draw students' attention to the openings for sample conversations and encourage students to use this as a model. • Students should take turns asking for and giving advice.

> **Answer key: Ex 1&2** Student A: A problem: fever/temperature/advice: go to bed B twisted ankle/advice: get an X ray C problem: insect bite/advice: put some cream on it.; Student B: A problem: hurt/twisted/broken arm/advice: go to the hospital (and get an X ray) B problem: toothache/advice: go to the dentist C problem: cut hand/advice: put a bandage on it

12C Adjective honeycomb

Aims: To practice adjectives with prepositions

Instructions: Ex 1 • Give each student a photocopy of the worksheet. • Draw students' attention to the first sentence. • Ask students to find *crazy about* on the honeycomb grid and to circle the phrase. • Have students read the other sentences and find and circle the adjective + preposition phrase on the grid. • Point out that the prepositions may be above, below, or next to an adjective, and that there is one three-word phrase on the grid; the others are all two-word phrases.

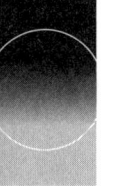

Answer key: 1 crazy about 2 proud of 3 scared of
4 famous for 5 similar to 6 bored with 7 interested in
8 fascinated by 9 different from

12D Consolidation Jumbo crossword puzzle

Aims: To review general vocabulary presented
throughout the book

Instructions: Ex 1 • Read the first clue for 1
Across to students. • Ask students to find 1
Across on the crossword and point out the number
of letters (6). • Ask the students to suggest the

solution (*gloves*). • Have students write the word
in the crossword. • Students should read the clues
and complete the crossword.

Answer key: Across: 1 gloves 7 scary
9 over 10 soccer 11 honey 12 tidy 15 memory
16 painkiller 17 Monday 18 graffiti
20 hairdresser 23 stepbrother 25 get married
27 overweight 29 uncle 30 bald 31 wear
32 spectators
Down: 1 good-looking 2 ocean 3 soap opera 4 library
5 smart 6 desert 8 racket 13 dishwasher
14 athletics 19 tie 21 score 22 leather 24 burglar
26 elbow 28 grated